ReLaT*Ive DiScoMFORT

RELATIVE DISCOMFORT

The Family Survival Guide

THE ESSENTIAL TOOL FOR LIVING THROUGH AND LAUGHING AT
ALL OF OUR FAMILY ENCOUNTERS

· JEREMY GREENBERG ·

**Andrews McMeel
Publishing, LLC**

Kansas City

08 09 10 11 12 MLT 10 9 8 7 6 5 4 3 2 1

ISBN-13: 978-0-7407-7376-1
ISBN-10: 0-7407-7376-3

Library of Congress Control Number: 2008923006

www.andrewsmcmeel.com

Attention: Schools and Businesses

Andrews McMeel books are available at quantity discounts with bulk purchase for educational, business, or sales promotional use. For information, please write to: Special Sales Department, Andrews McMeel Publishing, LLC, 1130 Walnut Street, Kansas City, Missouri 64106.

For Barbara. I love you, I will always love you, and there's not a damn thing you can do about it.

CONTENTS

PART IV

IF YOU'RE WATCHING THIS VIDEO, IT MEANS I'M DEAD AND YOU'VE JUST TURNED THIRTEEN

(SURVIVING BAR MITZVAHS, GRADUATIONS, AND BIRTHDAYS) · · · 63

PART V

YOU CAN NEVER GO HOME AGAIN

(BUT YOU CAN MOVE BACK IN WITH YOUR PARENTS) · · · 73

PART VI

PUBERTY, MENOPAUSE, AND OTHER EXCUSES FOR BEING A PAIN IN THE ASS · · · 85

PART VII

I WAS IN LABOR FOR FIFTEEN HOURS AND ALL I GET IS A CARD?

(SURVIVING MOTHER'S DAY AND FATHER'S DAY) · · · 97

PART VIII

WEDDINGS

(NOT JUST FOR GREEN CARDS ANYMORE) · · · 111

PART IX

GET ME SOME WARM BLANKETS AND A SHOTGUN

(SURVIVING HAVING A BABY) · · · 139

PART X

FAMILY REUNIONS, FIREWORKS, AND FAT RELATIVES WEARING THONG BIKINIS

(SURVIVING SUMMERTIME GET-TOGETHERS) · · · 151

PART XI
MY DADDY LIVES WITH THE CLEANING LADY NOW
(HOW TO HANDLE DIVORCES AND FAMILY SHIFTS) · · · 185

PART XII
OVER MY DEAD BODY
(SURVIVING FUNERALS) · · · 203

PART XIII
OH NO YOU DI-IN'T!
(SURVIVING FEUDS, FIGHTS, AND REALLY CRAZY SHIT) · · · 213

PART XIV
CONCLUSION · · · 223

PART

I

INTRODUCTION

chapter 1

INTRODUCTION

The family is the association established by nature
for the supply of man's everyday wants.

$\overline{\hspace{4cm}}$

· ARISTOTLE ·

Judging by the above quote, it's clear that Aristotle didn't have to
spend Thanksgiving listening to self-righteous Aunt Margaret tell
him that giving kids tap water is equal to child abuse. He didn't have
some stuck-up sister telling his wife that her kids would get a better
education playing in a junkyard than attending Montessori school.

If Aristotle had a mother-in-law who spent every family gathering
slurping Chardonnay until she felt comfortable enough to call her
husband a bastard, he would've recognized that the only "wants" our
families fulfill are those of wishing our mom would finally share her
recipe for peanut butter–Valium cookies—or at least make some for
herself. Sure, our families supply our "wants," if we count wanting
to fake our own death rather than sit through yet another cousin's
combination wedding/baby shower/high school graduation. Aristotle
would've realized what many of us already know: seeing family sucks.

It doesn't mean we don't love our relatives. They just become
annoying whenever we spend too much time with them. Holidays,

weddings, family reunions, births, graduations and birthdays, Mother's and Father's Day, and even funerals often become tests of endurance that would make climbing Everest seem like a walk in the park (provided that park is littered with fingertips and old ski goggles). What's needed is a tool for laughing off these annoyances, dealing with these crazy people, and having fun in the process. What's needed is *Relative Discomfort: The Family Survival Guide.*

The *Guide* is a collection of tips, tricks, games, and other helpful stuff to help you get through your upcoming family gathering. In addition to surviving major events, you'll learn how to move back in with your parents if you're no longer a kid, and how to kick your kid's ass back out of the house if you're a parent. You'll learn how to deal with pubescent and menopausal relatives—without the use of teargas. You'll discover the proper technique for a good Mother's Day or Father's Day guilt trip. And for kids of the guilt dealers, you'll find out how not to get suckered.

And just wait till you get to all the fun stuff in the divorce section, and the techniques for handling such insanities as fistfights and meltdowns! Unless you were born in a lab and then raised on the moon, you've got to read this book. Here's how:

HOW TO READ AND USE THE BOOK

1. *Begin by procrastinating.* After you've bought the book, don't read it. Set it next to all your other well-intentioned projects, like that half-knit baby blanket for the birth of your niece, who's now in seventh grade. Let the book sit somewhere and fester with the rest of your procrastinations, until you look up at the calendar and say, "Oh my god! In three days, I'll be face-to-face with the uncle who always tells me that I remind him of a cheerleader he dated in high school." (If you're a guy, that's

particularly alarming.) You'll know you're ready to read the book when you wake up in a cold sweat at the thought of having to politely refuse your stoner cousin's plea to help him invest in a Quiznos franchise. You'll have a knot in your stomach the size of Grandma Hanford's benign leg tumor. This book, your new best friend, will untie that knot for good.

2.   *Determine how much time you have.* If you're stuck in an airport or the waiting room of the free clinic, or you've just lost your job because of some new policy about hand washing, then you have time to read the entire book front to back.

    If you only have a few minutes before coming face-to-face with the reasons you moved to another part of the country, then go directly to the survival tips located at the end of each chapter. These are like inspirational quotes you'd find in a self-help book— except the demons they help you face are probably waiting to be picked up at the airport.

    In addition to the survival tips, another great solution for those short on time is to turn directly to the chapter that addresses what you expect will be your greatest challenge. For example, if you shudder at the thought of seeing that professor brother-in-law who considers the family reunion the perfect opportunity to make your SUV-driving relatives feel like monsters, turn to the chapter called "Red- and Blue-Staters (What to Do When the 'Two Americas' Show Up at the Same Family Reunion)." With just a quick read, you'll have the tools and confidence to slide away from debates about tax incentives for people who keep their cholesterol down, and go eat a fifth hamburger instead. Or let's say you'd like to know how to get through the holidays without having to wash a single dish. Turn to the chapter called "Dish Détente" and find everything you need for peacefully passing the buck.

wHEN To READ THIS Book

Here are a few particularly great times and places in which to read this book:

- *Read this book while breastfeeding.* If you have breasts or know someone who does, reading this book while lactating will fortify your milk with knowledge. The child suckling your udder is guaranteed to grow up to become a prominent member of society like a doctor, lawyer, or gangster rapper.
- *Read this book while going to the bathroom.* Putting something in your mind while removing something from your body maintains equilibrium.
- *Read this book while driving.* It's very dangerous to be on a cell phone while driving, so pick up a book instead. And if you cause an accident, at least no one can call you an idiot. After all, you were reading.
- *Read this book while your spouse is trying to talk to you.* Chances are, whatever he or she is about to say is covered somewhere in the book. If your wife asks, "Do you promise to have fun at my mom's house this year?" just reply, "Hold on. I'm reading the chapter on how to survive boring family visits."

Keep in mind that the information contained in this book is what's technically referred to as "highly effective bullshit." You'll find most of it isn't merely funny, but true, and useful in helping you have a better family encounter. However, some of this material is purely for entertainment. It's up to you to decide what will work for your brood, and what will land you behind bars, passing the time by writing angry letters to this author.

chapter 2

WHY WE HATE OUR FAMILIES
(EVEN THOUGH WE LOVE THEM)

You know that when I hate you, it is because I love you to a point of passion that unhinges my soul.

· JULIE DE LESPINASSE ·

. . . And my brother knows that when I hate him, it's because he once sold my bike to some kids at the bus stop, then told me it had been stolen.

Seeing family should be fun. We should eagerly anticipate reuniting with the people we've known our entire lives, eggnog-fueled laughter, the occasional soiled pants flung over the back porch to dry, catching two distant cousins making out in the basement; you know, the usual family fun. But we all know that picture of ease and comfort is a myth.

Why? Why does seeing family always fail to live up to our expectations? Why do we often find ourselves counting down the days of our family visit like it's time left on a prison term? If you've ever thought about snagging a spoon and trying to tunnel your way out of the house in the middle of the night just to avoid listening to one more debate about the amount of nuts in Aunt Nadine's fudge squares, then you understand why some people would rather be in a car crash than visit their relatives (at least then, if an airbag goes off, it'll save your life, not tell you the thread count of her new sheets). The reason why family gatherings don't live up to their billing is simple: We hate our families.

Yep, we hate 'em. It's official. We don't hate our families like we hate murderers, traffic jams, or musical theater. Those things are pure evil. Our families just irritate us, really. Seeing family is like catching a head cold: a temporary pain relieved by a snifter or four of brandy. If we understand and accept that it's possible to both love *and* hate our families, it'll go a long way in helping us tolerate, and maybe even enjoy their company.

SOME GOOD REASONS TO HATE YOUR FAMILY

Let's take a look at exactly what causes our relative discomfort:

Reason One: Our families remind us of what we would be like if our health insurance didn't cover counseling.

Do you have a racist uncle, a homophobic cousin (who for some odd reason also has a remarkable fashion sense), an arrogant brother, an obese aunt, an alcoholic mother, an overbearing father, and a perfect younger sister (and perfect in this case means being able to hide her bulimia from the rest of the family)? Of course you do. Every family since the beginning of time has some level of dysfunction. Heck, even Adam and Eve had personal problems. Right after Eve ate the apple, she ran to the bathroom and threw it up so she wouldn't get fat. The story goes that Adam and Eve learned they were naked and started to cover up, but the truth is Eve had body image issues, and used a fig leaf because she had no sweater to tie around her waist (of course, it was largely Adam's fault for telling Eve she could no longer fit behind the trees like she used to when they'd first met).

Many of us have taken great measures to evolve beyond the faulty thinking and bad habits of our families. We hate seeing them because they remind us of the people we were before we started attending Overeaters Anonymous and getting sensitivity training. Don't be surprised if, every December 24, you think about getting a sex-change operation just so your family will disown you. It's because you know that soon you'll be sitting next to the people who taught you that, unlike alcohol, you can still buy Nyquil after two A.M.

Reason Two: Our families are the most embarrassing people on earth (or under earth, should our folks be blind, hairless mole rats).

Very few people in this world have the power to make us flush with embarrassment quite like the people who share our last names and genetic risk for diabetes. Al Qaeda has yet to produce a video that can damage you like your father showing your fiancé(e) old home movies of you standing naked, peeing into the backyard swimming pool.

We learn of our family's power to embarrass us around the age when we attend junior high or high school. All of a sudden, there's that moment when you realize your mom's the only one who comes to the door with a chicken leg in one hand and a cigarette in the other. It is during these moments that you realize you must live a double life. You don't want the outside world to know your parents yell at the TV. You do whatever you can to keep your friends away from your dad and his government-conspiracy theories. You make up excuses for why they can't hang out at your house—everything from, "My house is being remodeled" to, "My younger sister is a famous child actor and doesn't like visitors." The last thing you need is your less-dysfunctional, "normal" friends noticing that your mom's hand is still stamped from last night's clubbing.

And all of us hope the embarrassment will stop when we become adults. We go off to college and learn a whole bunch of stuff we think will enlighten us and lift us above the dysfunctional antics of our families. However, when you show up at Thanksgiving or Christmas and your uncle tries to sell you life insurance *and* Tupperware at the same time, all our education, breathing techniques, and Pilates classes can't stop us from wondering if we'd have been better off being raised in a Serbian orphanage.

Unfortunately, there's still no cure for finding your family completely embarrassing. No matter how much we grow, we still can't believe we're related to people who clip their toenails at the dinner table.

Reason Three: Stupid is as stupid was raised.

A great reason to hate our family is we can blame them for any incorrect assumptions or stupid thoughts we have about the world. If your uncle tells you that the reason people hate each other in the Middle East is because their air has too many electrons, that's the kind of crap you're going to believe. When you get older, you will always be suspicious of people with Van De Graaff generators for causing all the hate in the world.

In short, anytime you think Democrats are communists, Man never really went to the moon, or that the Chinese have a secret plot to all jump off chairs at the same time and knock the earth out of orbit, you can thank your family for teaching you that nonsense.

Reason Four: Have you been disappointed in life? Guess whose fault that is? (Hint: They have pictures of you naked.)

A great reason to hate your family is when you're not getting what you want in life. Ever fail to get that promotion at work? That's your mom's fault for letting you stay home from school even though she knew you weren't sick. You were happy with your mom at the time, and the two of you ordered pizza, watched daytime TV, and talked about horses and the best kind of tampons to use on "heavy days." It was a fun, bonding moment. However, Julie, the other account rep, had a mother who made her go to school, even when she really was sick. When Julie asked her mom what the best kind of tampons were, she handed her a jar of blue liquid and said, "Find out for yourself." Julie spent a month researching and writing a report on maximum freshness and absorption while you played in the street and dreamed of being an extra in a John Cougar Mellencamp video. And now, as an adult, Julie doesn't occasionally call in sick to go to the movies like you do. She puts in the extra time and effort to make her PowerPoint presentation head and shoulders above your one-page pie graph.

Remember, although on some level we know our families love us and did the best they could, a big reason they annoy us, and part of why we "hate" them, is that we do blame them for our problems. Some part of us believes that "personal responsibility" is a myth propagated by crappy parents. It's just something they say so they can sleep at night instead of wondering if there's a connection between how fast they used to push you on the swing set and your recent bouts of vertigo.

Reason Five: In-laws: nature's reminder of why we suck.

When we see in-laws, we're on trial. In those first meetings with the family of your future groom or bride, you lose your identity. You are no longer Sharon or John, Tyrone or Shaniquah. You have no name. You are some stranger who has managed to start having sex with a member of their family. They want to know exactly what kind of cretin may get access to their DNA. When you first meet your mother-in-law-to-be and she asks, "So tell me about yourself," she's really saying, "Please explain what you think you can gain by sleeping with a member of my family."

Your entire relationship with in-laws is one of proving your right to exist. We hate extended family because we perceive them as (a) better than us/our family and therefore arrogant, or (b) less than us and therefore dragging our DNA back to the trailer park. If you're from a family that worked its way off a fishing boat in Norway to become doctors and teachers in Seattle, it's a step backward to have your daughter hook up with a guitar player she met at a bar around the corner from her college dorm. Your family holds a standard of education, and Keith the lead guitarist for Sporkupine says that his guitar and his GED (and your daughter) are all he needs. One of your highly cultivated purebreds has snuck off into the bushes with an alley mutt. And now, in one act of copulation, all those decades spent removing the smell of cod-liver oil from your clothes is wasted on a guy who brushes his hair only on days he has to go to court.

So every time we see our in-laws, we're either being reminded why we suck, or being challenged to demonstrate how we've grown out of the way we used to suck.

You Sure I'm Not Adopted?

By now you should be able to see your family in a new, dimmer light. You should no longer feel a tinge of guilt about wishing you could bury yourself in a spider hole rather than attend this year's festivities. In fact, if you can now say with confidence, "Yes, I hate my family," you are on your way to having a better family visit.

SURVIVAL TIPS

1. Our family members are like wild animals: they are just as scared of you as you are of them. The only difference is wild animals typically eat more quietly than our families.

2. We "hate" family because they are a constant source of embarrassment. Seeing them is like having broccoli in your teeth (except unlike our families, broccoli is healthy).

3. If you honestly think you can't stand to be around your in-laws for another minute, welcome to the family!

PART

II

GENERAL SKILLS FOR
ALL FAMILY GATHERINGS

chapter 3

ZOOS, PRISONS, AND OTHER PLACES TO PREPARE FOR THE SHOCK OF A FAMILY GATHERING

(PLUS OTHER FUN EXERCISES TO GET YOU INTO FAMILY-SEEING SHAPE)

Luck favors the mind that is prepared.

· LOUIS PASTEUR ·

. . . But nothing can prepare your mind for when Grandpa tells you about the first time he "got lucky."

Seeing family is like having to run a marathon after a year of sitting on your ass: it's a shock to the system. Normal life doesn't have twirling ballerina children, drunken uncles, stepfathers, and new wives all at once. Family gatherings can introduce many new elements simultaneously. If we aren't prepared, our system will crash.

The question is, "How do we prepare?" It's not like we can pay a group of strangers to annoy us (unless we go to dinner theater). Even if we could get someone to play the role of Aunt Henrietta and her unique parenting-by-shouting-f-words method, we still won't know for sure if she'll be the main cause of our event's craziness. It's impossible to know exactly what or who will make us pray our house catches fire just so we have an excuse for leaving the festivities early. What we can do is prepare ourselves emotionally and psychologically to deal with the inevitable shocks that come from seeing family.

This chapter is akin to that scene in *Rocky* when Sylvester Stallone's character is training for his fight by punching sides of beef in a meat locker. A frozen cow is much tougher to dent than Apollo Creed's face. Similarly, the five preparations in this chapter will have you ready to handle anything your family members might do to freak you out. We, too, are training to go the distance. No one wants to be knocked out in the third round by an uncle asking, "Which of you kids wants to see Unckie Frankie's vasectomy scar?"

#1 Environment

Whether you are from the city, country, or a suburb, if you're traveling to a different environment that you don't spend a lot of time in, it can be very shocking. Let's take a quick moment and review some great things we can do to prepare for these seldom visited places and the people who live there.

Hey, I'm Walking Here!

If you're from the country, sometimes big cities like New York, Chicago, or Atlanta can be more annoying than the family members you're visiting there. To prepare for your visit to a crowded, congested city, begin by packing all your animals into the barn. Try to use as many goats, oxen, and pigs as you can, since these animals do an excellent job of simulating New Yorkers and people from other large, devil-worshiping cities. Pack them in there really tight, then try walking from one end of the barn to the other. Notice how no one says, "Excuse me," and a few of them even pee on you. That is exactly what it's like to be in a big city. If you've got a pet sheep that can play the harmonica and beg for change, sit him at the entrance to the barn.

Y'all Talk Slower Than Molasses on Methadone

Visiting rural areas can often feel like you're spending several days in a slow-motion movie sequence. To get ready for seeing your country relatives, I recommend having conversations with anyone you know who has a stutter, cleft palate, or learning disorder. This will help you to keep from losing your mind when country cousin Carol eats up twenty minutes of your life describing the features of her new cordless telephone.

Another great way to prepare for being in the country is to start referring to your city's sewer system as "the creek." Country folk love their creeks. They play by them, carve their initials in trees that grow by them, and spend the summer days swimming in them until Maw rings the triangle, indicating that Paw is back from the general store and it's time for supper. Should you ever feel at a loss for conversation with your country relatives, you can always ask, "So how many crawdads are in your creek these days?"

Don't You Wish Your SUV Was Hot Like Mine?

Suburbs are probably the easiest foreign environments to visit, so long as you aren't a tree-hugging, housing sprawl–hating environmentalist; or one of those people who's into art, culture, and similar terrorist activities. If that describes you, the following little trick will help you see that suburbanites aren't just corporate robots, they're family:

Have you ever seen the look on Angelina Jolie's face when she's in Africa shopping for new children? She isn't disgusted because the

African village doesn't have a poetry night. She sees the place not as devoid of culture, but as having its own, unique culture. You must look upon your suburbanite relatives in the same way. The same pride an African chieftain feels about his brand-new banana-leaf codpiece is exactly what your suburban relatives feel about their new forty-foot, stainless-steel barbeque grill. Suburbanites are a simple yet beautiful people. We can learn a lot from them.

#2 VISIT THE ZOO

Do you know why those rare South American parrots at the zoo hide when you come over to their cage? It's because they're afraid you're going to ask them if they don't mind sharing a room with a bed-wetting nephew. One of the most humiliating aspects of seeing family is when we've got to spend our hard-earned vacation days stacked on top of aunts, cousins, and nephews. Just like animals at the zoo, we've been taken from our homes and forced to live in unnatural environments. However, we can look upon our animal brothers and sisters for perspective. If a proud beast like an elephant or lion can spend its entire life in captivity, you can surely survive three days and four nights pretending not to notice that your nana's house always smells like old Chinese food. If you ever begin to feel sorry for yourself because you're sharing a room with your six-year-old nephew and have to fall asleep staring up at a glow-in-the-dark solar system plastered on the ceiling, just think of that poor lion who has spent a lifetime pretending two trees and an unmowed lawn is the Serengeti.

#3 FIRING RANGES AND AIRPORT RUNWAYS

Some of our relatives talk way too loudly, or yell when they don't need to. It can be very uncomfortable to spend time with these people unless we condition ourselves to be just as annoying as they are. To prepare, begin by visiting the loudest place you can find. It can be an airport runway, firing range, or Italian neighbor's house. Then, try to carry on a conversation. If the person you're talking to can't hear you, raise your voice until he or she looks irritated. You will have found the volume at which your relatives speak. Continue speaking at this obnoxiously loud level right up until the time of the family gathering. This will guarantee that you won't find it disturbing or odd when your aunt bellows, "Hello, it's so nice to see you!!!" or "Does anyone want more carrots!!!?"

#4 PRISON

One of the things we typically aren't prepared for is the competition and sense of rivalry we have with family. That's why a visit to your local penitentiary is always a good idea. If you think there are painful power struggles among your relatives, try being forced to "share your bottom bunk" with a guy who insists you're his new pet poodle and will stab you if you make any noise other than "woof-woof." Any concerns about your environmentalist sister-in-law's calling you an animal because you work for a company with high carbon emissions will seem mild by comparison.

Prisoners also make the best of a place they don't want to be. Visiting them will help you do the same. Next time you think forcing yourself to eat one more bite of dry turkey is going to kill you, remember that some prisoner has just drunk three ounces of raisin-fermented, toilet-water prison gin—and liked it.

#5 Video Games

They say video games encourage violence among children. But what they don't tell you is what a good job video games do to prepare children *for* violence. If you wouldn't let your kids play a soccer game without stretching, you shouldn't take them to a large family event before they've conquered a few levels of *Grand Theft Auto.* Families can sometimes get into disturbing and painful fights. If your kid has been on a steady diet of *VeggieTales* and the Wiggles, he won't know what to think if the people he's known his entire young life suddenly start fighting and calling each other names. But a child who has spent years using simulated violence as a form of entertainment can simply be told that the adults are at level 1 of a new game called Make Aunt Stacy Cry, and must say and do hurtful things so they can make it to the no-one-is-talking-to-each-other bonus round. Keep in mind that kids play games in which they have to kill thirty or forty people/monsters to get to the next level. Not only will the child understand that the fighting and name-calling to be just a harmless game, but he may even haul off and call his auntie a poo-poo head just to play along.

Not So Shocking, Is It?

In just one short chapter, you've learned a bunch of fun things you can do to get yourself in family-seeing shape. While you are infinitely more prepared than you were, this is just the beginning!

SURVIVAL TIPS

1. Relatives from the country are slow, city folk are rude, and suburbanites have the cultural depth of bacteria. Prepare to accept their shortcomings. If done well, they'll think you like them, and they won't call you names after you leave.

2. If your relatives talk too loudly, it's typically because they are shouting over the voices in their heads.

3. If your family argues a lot, be sure to desensitize your child by having him play a lot of violent video games. Mommy's getting called a "hussy" is nothing to a child who spends his free time eviscerating Ninja peacekeepers.

chapter 4

PRE-GATHERING PREPARATION GAME: "REMEMBER WHEN"

(AS IN, "REMEMBER WHEN YOU TOLD YOUR MOM I WAS STUDYING TO BE A CHILD PSYCHOLOGIST AS AN EXCUSE FOR WHY I LIKE TO WATCH PROFESSIONAL WRESTLING?")

Truth springs from argument amongst friends.

· DAVID HUME ·

. . . And an argument amongst a husband and wife springs the truth that if only he'd married his cousin, he'd never have to worry about his wife getting along with his uncle.

For your upcoming visit, you may be asked to bring a dessert, your famous potato salad, or maybe even a box of fortified wine. But you will most definitely not be asked to bring bad memories and emotional baggage from past family gatherings. No one has ever said, "Please bring that amazing fruit salad of yours, and show up still angry about the time I made your husband cry by calling him a sissy." This is a new year. It's time to create fun new wounds, not pick at old ones. To help leave bad memories behind, nothing beats a good old-fashioned game of Remember When.

Playing the game is fun and easy. In fact, many of us have already played Remember When without even knowing it. To begin, you or your partner brings up something from the past like, "Remember when you got too drunk and sculpted your mashed potatoes into the shape of a vagina?" Now it's your spouse's turn. She'll say something like, "Yeah, remember, that was the time you didn't warn me that your father was planning on asking me to convert to Judaism." Then it's player one's turn again: "Speaking of fathers, remember when yours told you that the neighbor boy you had a crush on all through high school is single again, right in front of my face?"

The game is played until someone cries, threatens to turn the car around, or yells, "Yeah, well, you're an asshole!" (Note: If you don't have a partner, by all means feel free to play Remember When against the voices in your head. However, if you're driving, please abstain from having make-up sex.)

THE BENEFITS OF PLAYING REMEMBER WHEN

Why would we *want* to fight with our spouse? Because you love them, that's why. Just take a look at what we gain from rehashing bad memories:

(a) It helps our spouse understand why, when it comes to seeing his or her relatives, we're as anxious as a dog at bath time (an anxiety that our country relatives may not be familiar with).

Often, our partner doesn't always understand why we'd rather get a benign tumor than spend three days with his or her family (although if you think about it, unlike some of your relatives, at least tumors have the ability to grow). Your husband or wife may have grown up with these people, but when you see his or her relatives, it's basically like walking into a crowded restaurant, sitting down at a table of strangers, and being told, "Those people are now family. You've got to love them no matter how much they swear, how often they keep asking you to hold your tongue while spelling 'Mississippi,' or how many of their political conversations end with, 'See, that's why there should be an electric chair in every Wal-Mart.'"

Playing Remember When helps your spouse understand how to protect you from his or her family. For example, during the game you might say, "Remember when you told your mom I only have one ball?" She may at first deny it, saying, "I never told her you have one ball. What gave you that idea?" And you say, "When she served a plate of appetizers, she looked at me dead in the eyes and said, 'Shrimp balls? Would you like two, or will one ball be enough?'"

It doesn't matter if she cops to spilling the beans about your balls. She now knows that you don't like her and her mom discussing your testicles, and she can remedy the problem. This year she can tell her mom she was joking or angry with you when she said that. Or she could even restore your ego with a final bragging comment about the incredible powers that one ball has, just to set the record straight. She'll stand up and proudly say, "My husband can ride a bicycle longer than anyone we know!"

(b) Remember When lets you and your spouse get *your* argument out of the way, so you can focus on arguing with the people you only see once a year.

There's nothing more insensitive than traveling across the country just to accuse your husband of hating you because he "forgot" to pack that festive, reindeer-pattern sweater you gave him last year. You and your spouse can piss each other off anytime you want. Family gatherings should be used to piss off those loved ones you only see once a year.

Remember When is great for getting you and your spouse's fight out of the way. Ideally, you should start fighting with each other on the drive or flight to the family gathering (or while waiting for your guests to arrive, if you're the host).

While playing Remember When, get the argument flowing by redirecting all comments into a personal attack. For example, if your spouse asks, "Remember when your mother said I was a pretty good cook for a peasant girl?" you should respond with, "I'm just surprised she hasn't said anything about how you hold up your side of conversations by constantly saying, 'No shit, really?'"

You will notice the personal attack didn't have anything to do with the "peasant girl" comment. By all means, toss any rude comment into the ring that can get a good argument going. If you love your spouse and want them to have a relaxing, peaceful family visit, you won't hesitate to ask them if this year, they wouldn't mind controlling their flatulence (even if they have none).

GAME COMPLETION

When do you know your game of Remember When is done? If you ask a simple question like, "Maybe we should take the kids to the zoo?" and get a response like, "How about instead, we find a public park to have sex in," the game is over. There is no longer a need to remind each other of past hurts or start a fight. Now it's time to prepare for fighting with the people you're about to see. You can ask, "Uncle Steve's going to be there, right?" to which your spouse might reply, "Yes. Have you ever noticed that Uncle Steve always smells like corn chips? Let's bring him a bag of Fritos with his name on it. I think he'll like that."

SURVIVAL TIPS

1. Don't force a game of Remember When. It will occur naturally once the stress of the travel combines with the anxiety of having to spend several days declining requests to arm-wrestle various cousins.

2. If you happen to be in an airport or other public place while playing Remember When, argue as loudly as possible. You want everyone around you to see that you're committed to having a better family visit. They'll be so impressed, they'll probably stop and stare (and if they tell their kids not to watch you, it's just because they don't want to seem like bad parents by comparison).

3. If you think your kids are mature enough to be part of the fight, by all means allow them to join the game. It's actually quite adorable to hear a kid ask, "Remember when I asked Grandma why her veins run on the outside of her skin?"

chapter 5

BORING FAMILY VISITS
(HOW TO KEEP FROM FALLING INTO A COMA)

This is the curse of our age,
even the strangest aberrations
are no cure for boredom.

· STENDHAL ·

. . . And, for many of us, there are no stranger
aberrations than our relatives.

Anyone who thinks Christmas really lasts for twelve days probably spent one day at a really boring Christmas and got confused. Some family events can move so slowly, we feel like spiking the food with Dexedrine just to see what will come of it (probably a new world record in post-meal dishwashing). Either the activities are not our idea of fun, or we're stuck in the middle of a conversation about deciduous plants and wishing we were also dormant during this part of the year. Yet unlike a dumb movie or a bad date, you can't just ask for your money back and leave. Your spouse has probably warned you ahead of time to be on your best behavior or risk some form of future pain. Pretending to have food poisoning just so you can leave the table early will probably violate that verbal contract.

What can you do to keep from being bored off your ass? Alcohol may seem like the answer, but drunk relatives may just go from boring to obnoxiously boring. Plus, if you're drunk, the chances of your breaking the contract are much higher.

TOOL TIME

In the fight to stay conscious, we have two main tools:

1. *The Distraction:* We can play games to distract ourselves like, "Which Relative Has the Worst Fashion Sense?" or analyze boring family members for information about their personal lives (e.g., Pretending your sixty-year-old aunt's fascination with unicorns is a sign that she might be a sex addict).

2. *The Changer:* Here we actually try to change the conversation or activity from boring to interesting. If the plan is to go hiking, a good conversation about recent snakebites and mountain-lion attacks may help people realize how much fun it would be to go to the movies instead.

Let's look at a few common activities and conversations that could potentially bore the hell out of us, followed by some suggested ways to use the above tools.

Dessert Intermission Conversation

Your Aunt Danielle, known affectionately by her family and anything black in her wardrobe as Aunt Dandruff, has one saving grace: incredible chocolate mousse cake (sprinkled with flecks of powdered sugar). It's all you can think of. But for some reason, the family decides to sit there and discuss the epidemic of juvenile diabetes rather than clear the table.

The Distraction: Stare at people's mouths as they speak. Try to figure out who has the most cavities, based on light reflecting off fillings. Then when dessert finally is served, see if there's a connection between Cavity Mouth and the number of slices of cake he or she eats.

The Changer: Your goal is to get cake and get it now. Just stand up and start cleaning the table. Ask Aunt Dandruff if she'd like you to plate up the cake. She probably doesn't want anyone messing with her masterpiece and will make sure she beats you back to the kitchen. Dessert is served.

TV Watchers and Book Readers

No one drives 200 miles to sit with relatives and watch the History Channel. Hopefully, there'll be a show about the Irish Potato Famine to spark a discussion between your half-English/half-Irish family.

The Distraction: A great one for sedentary, noninteractive family is the "earlobe beauty contest." Sit in the back of the room and study each relative's earlobes for size, thickness, and distance from the skull. They say large and thick earlobes are a sign of intelligence. See if this holds true for your family. Is your earlobe-endowed relative as smart as her triple-pierced ears indicate, or would some of those earlobe cells have been better used on her frontal lobe?

The Changer: Your goal is to have the TV turned off and/or the books put down. To accomplish this, set off the smoke alarm. Not only will you startle your family and send them running into the front yard, but you'll be able to make sure that the household is ready when there's a real fire. Besides, now you're free to ask, "Since we're outside, who's up for a game of rugby?"

Activities You Don't Want to Do

Disneyland has been on the calendar since the big family visit was scheduled a year ago. However, the thought of holding your nephew's cotton candy all day while he goes on rides isn't appealing. It's the worst kind of boring—not having fun while thousands of organisms around you are.

The Distraction: Conduct an experiment. See how much cotton candy it takes for the kids to realize the rides aren't as much fun as going home and taking a nap.

The Changer: Planned family events like this are very often difficult to change. In these situations, it may be worth risking the ire of your spouse by pretending to have stomach flu, sprained ankle, or recently developed fear of crowds (that for some reason didn't affect you two nights ago, when everyone went to the movies). They'll probably know you're just avoiding spending the day as a living coat rack, but it just might be a price you have to pay.

No, I'm Listening

If we're willing to use our imaginations, even the slowest, dullest family visit can be bearable. The next time you're forced to spend three days watching your relatives knit, just pretend that you're overseeing a third-world sweatshop. You can even yell, "Keep knitting, Nana! You're at this Thanksgiving to be emotionally distant and make blankets, not to talk."

SURVIVAL TIPS

1. Sometimes, we think we'll die from boredom if we spend one more hour sitting on a beach with our relatives. However, if we use our imaginations to pretend that a tidal wave could hit at any time, it can be a lot more fun (though they'll probably ask why you're sunbathing with your running shoes on).

2. If you want to live dangerously, you can try to get out of conversations or activities by pretending to be sick, or have allergies or phobias. (However, the death-of-a-loved-one excuse probably won't fly.)

3. If it seems like *everything* your relatives do is boring, there's a good chance they've all started attending Alcoholics Anonymous. Be supportive of their new lifestyle, even though they're no longer cool.

PART

III

IT'S THE MOST WONDERFUL TIME OF THE YEAR

(UNLESS YOU'VE GOT TO SPEND IT WITH BITCHY AUNT MARGARET)

chapter 6

ARRIVAL STRATEGIES

Showing up is 80 percent of life.

———————————————————

· WOODY ALLEN ·

. . . Showing up without pissing anyone off
is the other 20 percent.

One of the most overlooked parts of the family gathering is the
arrival. Like a gymnastics competition, you can do all your
flips perfectly, but if you land wobbly the routine is ruined. Years of
not ovulating have gone for nothing just because you screwed up one
small detail. The same is true of your big family gatherings. If your
arrival isn't perfect, all your preparing to not be annoyed by your
Christian Stoner cousin is wasted. It won't matter that you've been
prepared to block out his stories about how he's sure Jesus smoked
pot because he was so peaceful and always turning stuff into food.
If you accidentally insult your hostess, watching that uncoordinated
niece with chronic ear infections try and perform her dance recital
will be the least of your pains.

The key to a successful arrival strategy is ingratiating yourself to the host. This may mean showing up early, pretending to like bland food, or helping with chores you don't want to do. Unfortunately, having a better holiday may mean kissing a little mother-in-law ass (that is, little by comparison to one of Saturn's moons); or sucking up to your rich dentist brother's trophy wife. To help us endure this humiliation, let's remind ourselves what we can gain with a good arrival strategy:

Sleeping Arrangements

Do you want the spare bedroom so you can sleep with your wife's collection of childhood stuffed animals, or do you want to sleep on the couch next to the fireplace mantel and Grandpa David's ashes? Our host controls where we sleep. They are the captain of the ship and can determine if we get the nice hammock with the parrot and a bottle of rum, or if we have to sleep down in the galleys propped against the bilge pump. Family gatherings are an endurance sport. You will last a lot longer if people don't have to walk by you at night to pee.

However, if you get stuck on the couch, it's your right to raid the liquor cabinet and the leftovers as much as you want, and at whatever hour you choose. If they didn't want you to get drunk at three in the morning, they would have set up the inflate-a-bed in the back office.

Mealtime Seating Chart

Do you want to sit next to your college-age younger cousin, and hear all the latest techniques for how to get tequila stains out of a Wonder Bra; or do you want to listen to Great Aunt Betty trying to time her cheesecake bites in between each emphysema wheeze? Family gatherings are always a lot less painful if we're sitting next to someone who doesn't gross us out. Our host controls where we sit, including who must sit at the proverbial kids' table. Forming the right bond with your host can mean the difference between staring at a reminder of how great twenty-two-year-old breasts are, or being asked to help little drooling Jimmy cut up his turkey. (Note: Sometimes it's actually beneficial to sit at the kids' table if it's in your best interest to avoid all the adults.)

Inheritance

Family gatherings are about more than who can go the longest without crying. Not being a pain in the ass during the holidays can make the difference between being willed the summer condo in San Diego, or the "heirloom" lamp your grandfather made during arts-and-crafts time at the nursing home.

ARRIVING EARLY

Sometimes it's worth packing your bags the night before, just so you can make it to Grandma Dee's house a few hours before the rest of the family. Especially if you know your professor brother-in-law will be there, and one of his favorite pastimes is making you feel like the family idiot because you dropped out of college to work in the construction industry. Any bond you can make with the host will nestle you tightly within the family herd, and keep you from getting picked on by the hyenas.

However, be smart when arriving early. Never say, "Do you want me to help you finish cleaning?"

What you're really saying is, "This house is filthy! I've seen cleaner homes in Hurricane Katrina footage." Even if your intentions are good and you don't mean to be insulting, it's always best to pretend the house is immaculate, even if it's filthy enough to qualify as a superfund sight.

In fact, some hosts hate when people arrive early. They need every last minute to conceal their smoking habit, stash their porno, and toss empty ice-cream cartons over the back fence. If you arrive early and it's clear you have intruded on your host's effort to hide her private life of debauchery from the rest of the family, tell her that you forgot something and ask where the nearest store is. Hide there till it's safe to return.

If you should arrive while your host is still cleaning but doesn't appear annoyed that you showed up, be sure to help. Of course you don't want to, but keep in mind that twenty minutes of vacuuming could mean the difference between sleeping in a room with a real bed or sharing a barf-infused futon with the cat. Do whatever's necessary to reduce your host's stress. If that means cleaning, help clean. It could just mean listening to stories about what a bitch Veronica at work is. Sometimes all you have to do to put your host at ease is admire her paintings, letting her know that those classes she's taking at the community center are really paying off. Keep in mind that with every polite nod, you are making the next three days of your life much less miserable.

What If I Can't Arrive Early?

If you know you should arrive early but end up being late, try not to make a big deal out of it. Whatever you do, don't show up and say, "I see you've started to drink without us." If your host is already drunk, she probably felt incredible anxiety over family visiting her home. Calling attention to the fact she's already dipped into the cooking sherry will reflect just as poorly on you as it does on her. After all, if you weren't going to visit, she wouldn't have to get drunk.

Arriving Late

Sometimes it makes sense to arrive late. If you and your host have an open, existing relationship based on mutual hatred, then it makes no sense for you two to endure each other more than you have to. Also, arriving late will make sure the rest of the family is already there to run interference between you and your adversary. Don't be so late that it's disrespectful and you disrupt the holiday; just be late enough so you don't have to help set the table. Since there's no chance of sitting in the good spot or sleeping in the good bed, don't bother showing up with wine or dessert. If you really want to bring something for this relative, put a bow on an unwrapped self-help book, hopefully with the title *Women Who Grudge Too Much.*

Your Presnap Read

If you are going to your parents' house for the holiday, you are probably well aware that the best way to piss your mom off is to pull out the broom that her dog thinks is the devil, waving it in the air until little Max barks maniacally and foams at the mouth. However, many of us are meeting potential in-laws for the first time this holiday, or we're going over to rich "Aunt Fat and Uncle Happy's" new suburban McMansion. We know much less about these people, and must quickly figure out how to keep them from hating us.

There is a term in football called a "presnap read," where the quarterback looks at the defense to determine what play to run. A good arrival strategy also includes a presnap read, but this read is just to make sure we know enough about our host to keep them from snapping.

Presnap Reads

- *Taking your shoes off:* Does your host make you take your shoes off? Taking your shoes off, like prison sex, is all about power. It's like when the doctor makes you get naked just to check your blood pressure. Keeping dirt off the rug is just what they tell you so you'll play by their rules. A hostess or host who makes you take your shoes off is one step away from insisting that all men pee sitting down. They need you to respect them and their home.

Joking with this host by saying something like, "Wow, the food smells great—did you get Applebee's curbside to go?" will probably get your inflate-a-bed set up in the dog run.

■ *Coat room vs. closet:* Where do they throw your stuff? If your host carefully hangs your coat in the closet, that means you'd better refold your towel in the bathroom (and refold that towel perfectly. None of that "in half" crap. Tri-fold that thing, and do it right!).

This host values order. You are liable to ruin her sense of self-worth if you use the wrong fork with salad. If you don't use a coaster, this person may slip a scorpion into your duvet cover! Disregard this host's neuroses at your peril.

However, someone who takes your coat and carelessly launches it into the back bedroom from the hallway will become thoroughly annoyed with you if you ask for a glass with your soda or beer. "Just drink out of the can—we're family!" Make sure to keep it informal with a bedroom coat-thrower.

Final Note on Bringing Food and Drink

The last concern we will address regarding arrivals is bringing food and drink. Here are just a few basic ground rules:

■ Showing up with wine is nice. Showing up with beer says, "I ran out of Vicodin."

■ Only bring a dessert if specifically requested. Showing up with an apple pie that's better than the host's is an act of war.

■ If a host says not to bring anything, that means pick something up at the store. If a host says bring something small, start cooking now! You are responsible for providing half the meal.

SURVIVAL TIPS

1. Arrive early, so everyone who shows up after you feels like an outsider.

2. Taking your shoes off is a tactic used by Guantanamo Bay guards to control the prisoners.

3. Take care not to make backhanded comments. Saying things like, "Your house smells great, is that lavender? I can hardly tell you have a dog," is a huge mistake. You may be trying to pay a compliment, but all your host will hear is that her home smells like her dog ate some flowers, then took a crap in the air vent.

chapter 7

SHOWING UP ALREADY DRUNK OR HIGH

(WHEN IS IT A GOOD IDEA, AND WHEN IS IT ABSOLUTELY NECESSARY?)

Man seeks to escape himself in myth.

· JEAN COCTEAU ·

. . . Man seeks to escape his family in Michelob.

A holiday gathering is like an Olympic event. While competitive athletes train, eat healthily, and take care of themselves, there's one thing that separates the professional from the amateur: performance-enhancing substances. Important events like the Three-Day, Don't-Call-Your-Mom-a-Bitch Relay require a little "doping" to make sure we don't let our country down.

Don't worry if you think you'll need a little help from some "friends" before this year's holiday. Chances are, the first time your mom saw you, she was on enough painkillers to detusk an elephant. It's okay if you need something to handle seeing her.

Let's review a few cases in which you should definitely come to the holiday either buzzed, or having baked something other than your famous Potatoes au Gratin:

(a) If you know the host is culinarily challenged, being stoned or drunk will help you chew your food without making faces.

Everyone knows that certain wines go with certain foods. Drink a Cabernet with steak, a Chardonnay with fish. Well, the same is true with bad food. If you know from past experience that your hostess assassinates every dish with enough Hungarian paprika to color a Chinese flag, choose the appropriate alcoholic beverage ahead of time.

Recommended predrinking list for certain foods:

- *Dry turkey:* Eating this is a tough task; you'll want to be as numb as possible. Try a hard alcohol like Jack Daniel's. But be careful not to have too much. There is a fine line between being relaxed enough to swallow baked breast of drywall, and being so drunk you don't mind telling the cook that if she'd left the turkey in the oven any longer, she could've served it from an urn.
- *Cold or dry roast beef:* Before sitting down to a nice, frigid, desiccated side of beef, tune yourself up with some malt liquor. Malt liquor can often sneak up on someone and surprise him by how drunk he is. Hopefully, it will sneak up on you right after your host says, "This recipe is so good, I didn't even make gravy."
- *Too-salty ham:* If you've been served a ham that rivals the Dead Sea in salt content, you're going to want to go for a dessert wine. Port and other fortified wines are so sweet that they can quickly burn out taste buds. Not only will you be wasted, your tongue will be too tired to notice that it's being brined.

(Note: Don't worry about enduring slimy green beans, cold mashed potatoes, or stuffing that would be better used to insulate heating ducts. If a side dish sucks, just don't eat it.)

(b) If the family is Irish or Russian, chances are, there won't be enough booze to go around, so you're better off priming the pump beforehand.

Nightmares of sitting down for breakfast only to learn that your older sister has eaten all the Cheerios can replay themselves if you don't take care to lube up beforehand. Even if your family isn't Russian, Irish, or alcoholic, chances are, they do drink more than usual during the holidays. If you're bringing over a new boyfriend or girlfriend to meet your folks this year, it can look really bad to have a bunch of family fighting for the last drop of scotch. Show some class: hide some scotch in an empty Snapple bottle and drink it on the way over.

(c) If your host thinks that drinking in front of the kids is wrong, showing up already drunk respects her house rules.

Many people do not feel that having alcohol around kids is appropriate. These high-strung control freaks are usually the ones we need alcohol to endure. So if you know it's going to be a holiday with Teletubbies on the TV, and repeated requests to "Please stop calling my four-year-old 'Homeboy,'" you'd better show up already needing a designated driver.

RECOMMEND USES FOR OTHER DRUGS DURING THE HOLIDAYS

This book doesn't condone illegal drug use, but it would be delinquent in its preparation if it didn't discuss where other drugs fit in with the holidays.

- *LSD or mushrooms:* These psychedelics can make this Easter the first time you'll be glad the kids paint eggs. Let the colors wash away the fact that your aunt is sitting pissed off in the corner, trying to tell everyone that this day isn't about eggs or bunnies. Of course it isn't; it's about taking a trip through reality, man.

- *Meth:* Meth is a Chanukah drug. How else are you going to stay up for eight straight days and nights? Meth is also a great drug for Yom Kippur (the Jewish day of fasting). And when all your teeth fall out, you'll finally have a good excuse for not having to eat gefilte fish. (Note: gefilte fish is poached day-old carp eaten by Jews who didn't think the Holocaust was painful enough. It's fucking gnarly!)

- *Crack:* Shame on those of you who thought of Kwanzaa. Crack is a Christmas drug and essential when one goes caroling for orange soda.

- *Heroin:* Many rock stars have been resurrected from a heroin overdose after having been clinically dead for three minutes. One good resurrection deserves another—Happy Easter!

- *Marijuana:* This one's a no-brainer (something potheads should be used to). The Native Americans used hemp to make jewelry and rope (and occasionally to make Paranoid Dove check his teepee for snakes every five minutes). By smoking it on Thanksgiving, you are honoring their memory (and what's left of yours).

A Few Notes on when To Show Up Sober

- *Many dysfunctional families bond through boozing.* If you get wasted beforehand, they may feel offended: "What, you're too good to kill brain cells with the rest of the family?" You need not worry about running out of spirits with these families. As far as they

are concerned, Thanksgiving is the day we remember how the
Native Americans taught us how to turn corn into grain alcohol.

■ *Another time to show up sober is if you're traveling to see in-laws
who've got a tradition of a premeal football game or other athletic
activity.* Your vertical leap can't help your team win if you're puking in the bushes.

Last Call

Please be responsible when drinking this holiday. Do the mature
thing at your holiday gathering: get so drunk, you pass out on the
couch. Not only won't you drink and drive, you may even provide a
fun new family story for next year.

Survival Tips

1. It's okay to use substances to accomplish your goals (such as surviving
    the holidays). Who broke the home-run record: Barry Bonds or Barry
    Manilow?

2. There's a long tradition of combining alcohol with holiday food. Eggnog
    began with someone's trying to liven up a dull pudding. We may soon be
    drinking glasses of roast-beef bourbon.

3. If you don't drink or use drugs, you can still accomplish the same goals
    of this chapter by showing up to the holiday with a plate of Maui-Wowi
    brownies. People who can't feel their arms won't notice if your elbows
    are on the table.

4. You don't need to drink ahead of time if your family bonds through booze
    (unless you find your family more annoying than they find you).

chapter 8

CHILDREN DURING THE HOLIDAYS
(HOW TO HAVE FUN AT THEIR EXPENSE)

Children make you want to start life over.

· MUHAMMAD ALI ·

. . . Without the children

Some people say that the holidays are a magical time for children, but the truth is that children make the holidays a magical time for adults. Their playful spirit, wild imagination, and ability to play make-believe can all be used to make this year a very special holiday—for us.

Up till now, your holidays have probably been one-sided. You buy presents for your children, and in return they give you a picture their teacher *made* them draw. They get an Xbox, and you get evidence that your child has the artistic talent and vision of a county-fair chicken. If we're to have a holiday that reminds us why we stopped using birth control, we need some fun new games and activities.

HE HAS THE MIND OF A CHILD

Before we get to the good times, let's remember that children have
the magical ability to make anything fun. For example, in the mind of
a child, painting Easter eggs is just as much fun as painting a house.
And kids love to play on ladders! Not only do you give the kids a
rare holiday treat, you'll get some projects done. This is the kind of
gift our children can share with us. Gone will be the days of having
to force a smile for yet another handful of sloppily written coupons
"good for one free cleanup after dinner."

ACTIVITIES AND GAMES (FOR THE KIDS)

The following is a mixture of activities that are educational, produc-
tive, or just darn fun:

- *You can entertain young children for hours with the game "Which
  Ornaments Are Edible?"* Remember, young kids experience the
  world through their mouth. If you get tired of ornaments and
  want a great bonding moment, nothing beats a tasting tour of
  the tool shed (because who hasn't wondered if a hammer tastes
  different than a wrench?).

  You can also play the game "Which Ornaments Aren't
  Edible?" but it doesn't last as long.
- *Teach your kids your own holiday traditions*, like the one in which,
  after the kids open the presents, Mommy and Daddy resell them
  on eBay.

  If they really want that PlayStation, they can place a bid like
  everyone else. Just be sure that the tradition doesn't include their
  having a PayPal account with their parents' credit card number.

- *If your hostess insists on having a cat box in plain sight, you can play the great word-association game "Turkey or Shit."* This game is great for building comparative-reasoning skills (however, incorrect answers may upset your hostess).
- *Another fun game that builds a child's creativity is coming up with nicknames for family members.* If Uncle Tommy is overweight, teach a kid to call him Uncle Tummy. For you to say this would be rude, but kids don't know any better.

Chanukah is a celebration of a little bit of oil lasting eight days, when really it should've lasted for just one (it's kind of like having a holiday for a rental car that got surprisingly good gas mileage). Should a child ask her mother why she has to make one piece of candy last a week, tell her she's celebrating Chanukah.

Kwanzaa is the celebration of the year's first harvest. What better excuse to send your children into the yard with a rake to harvest all the leaves. If your kids try to give you some excuse, like telling you they aren't African American, just hand them the rake and tell them that you believe in living in a color-blind society.

- *Take your kids shopping with you,* and let them know that if they find a toy they like, they should start crying loudly and yelling, "Mommy, a stranger tried to grab me!" It's usually good for at least a 10 percent discount.
- *Kids often love to hear stories.* Let them hear the story about "The Child Who Loved to Do Dishes" and "The Princess and the Swiffer." A great one right before company arrives is "Spic 'N Spanderella," about a girl who mops the floor so well that her reflection comes to life and becomes her playmate (until one day when her brother tracks in dirt and she magically disappears).

CHILD LABOR IS A DEROGATORY TERM FOR ELVES

Just try a few of these games and see if they don't renew your holiday spirit. Gone will be the fears of children as sugar-doped psychopaths running through the house knocking over lamps and pulling down curtains. This holiday, they'll be Santa's little helpers.

SURVIVAL TIPS

1. Our children just want to interact with us, no matter if we're making cookies or whipping up a batch of cement to level a walkway.

2. Do be careful when enjoying your child's assistance. For example, if your son's begging you to let him iron your clothes, make sure he first repairs the stepladder that he'll need to reach the ironing board.

3. Let's teach kids that the real spirit of the holidays is giving, by having them give us a hand.

chapter 9

CHEAPSKATE SANTA
(OR MISERLY MOSHE FOR MY JEWISH PEEPS)

Talk is cheap.

· OLD PROVERB ·

. . . Unless you call it a seminar.

Why stress out about buying gifts this holiday when, with a little ingenuity, you can come out having spent little or no money? Before we get to the exact strategies and tips for coming out ahead, let's review some good reasons to be the "cheap one" this holiday.

SOME GOOD EXCUSES/REASONS TO SAVE YOUR DOUGH

- *What if your family's evil?* Do you really want to reward people who counterfeit handicap-parking permits with new travel mugs and iTunes gift certificates?

■ *What if a member of the family hates you?* What's the right gift for someone who thinks that her brother made a mistake by marrying you? Even if you try to take the high road and get her something that she can connect with (like an iguana), chances are, she'll criticize whatever you get her with a sarcastic, "Oh, *this* is nice." Why spend money on your own abuse?

■ *What if you've recently quit your job to walk the earth in sandals?* How can you impose vain materialism on your family (not to mention that you've spent your last dime on some kick-ass Birkenstocks)?

■ *What if you aren't that close to the family?* You can't just give them a gift certificate—that would be an admission that you know nothing about them. Even worse, you could end up getting a diabetic relative a box of Godiva chocolates. Your kind gesture may send you scrambling to her purse to find the insulin.

■ *What if your kids actually* have *been naughty?* Rewarding them with gifts screws up Santa's balance of power. Plus it sends the wrong message. If your kid got suspended from school for fighting, buying him the 2008 version of Rock 'em Sock 'em Robots is practically encouraging him to train for his next schoolyard bout.

■ *What if you've just gotten your credit back on track and have even started making small monthly payments on your BlueHippo computer?* You know that buying your kid a Fisher-Price keyboard is a gateway purchase to buying a thousand-dollar electric guitar for yourself. If your kid asks why he can't have his keyboard, tell him it's because Daddy's music days are over.

THE BEST THINGS IN LIFE ARE FREE
(OR AT LEAST INEXPENSIVE)

Let's begin by looking at some nifty ways of handling a kid's Christmas on the cheap.

Kids

- *Coupons:* Kids love to give those coupons offering free chores. Why not take a page out of their book and give a coupon for a "free, one-hour life-skills seminar" (a $150 value!)? Life skills can include anything from how to convincingly call in sick to work, to pretending to be mentally challenged so the family can pre-board on the flight home. Make sure that the seminar comes with a certificate of completion so they don't feel cheated on their gift.
- *In-store credit:* If you own a business, give gift certificates for *your* business. Don't worry; eventually, an eight-year-old will need twenty-five dollars' worth of ceiling fans.
- *School supplies:* Kids always need pens and notepads for school. They might say "Kinko's" on them, but remember, they're not just receiving free crap you've gotten by making a three-cent copy. They're getting high-quality, name-brand items.

Adults

For the adults we must shop for, here are some wonderfully inexpensive "gifts":

- *The gift of giving:* Hand them a letter stating that you've donated money on their behalf to a charity. If they ask which charity, tell them knowing would ruin the gift.
- *Give a magazine subscription:* It usually takes four to six weeks for the first issue to arrive. That's more than enough time for them to forget, and for you to cancel the subscription.

- *Lost and found gifts:* The next time you're at an amusement park, skating rink, homeless shelter, or anywhere else that has a well-stocked lost and found, be sure to look for a pair of socks or an old hat that might fit your dad. If he asks why they're dirty, old, and smelly, just say that's the latest fashion. Now he smells like the cool kids.

- *Potluck:* This isn't so much a gift idea as a general tip for saving some money. If you're ever invited to a potluck-style party, always volunteer to bring the napkins or silverware. You'll find many grocery stores, sandwich shops, and so on that offer free plastic forks, knives, straws, or napkins (and for future reference, department-store bathrooms offer free rolls of toilet paper to people who bring their own backpacks). Not only will you have made your contribution to the potluck, you won't feel weird helping yourself to a second serving of your sister's handmade veal ravioli.

I THINK YOU DROPPED A QUARTER

This year, show your family your thoughtfulness and creativity by giving them gifts they would never think to get: like stacks of cardboard coasters you've taken from a Chili's. Sure, you had to buy a Diet Coke to get them. But the look on their face when you hand them folded napkins full of brand-new unused coasters will be worth every penny.

SURVIVAL TIPS

1. We love our families, but that doesn't mean we've got to spend a year paying 18 percent in credit-card interest to prove it.

2. When buying newspapers, always be sure to grab the entire stack. For a mere quarter, you can stay informed while stocking up on wrapping paper. You'll even have a Port-A-Potty for the young'uns on long drives!

3. If you want to add some additional excitement to a child's present, get him an unopened Coke or Pepsi bottle during one of their million-dollar contests. Not only will he get a delicious soda this Christmas, he'll get the chance to win a Jet Ski or thousands of other great prizes. (This tip is void where prohibited by law.)

chapter 10

DISH DÉTENTE
(HOW TO ALMOST HELP WITH THE DISHES, AND OTHER TRICKS FOR APPEARING TO BE HELPFUL WHILE REALLY NOT LIFTING A FINGER)

The best intelligence test is what we do
with our leisure.

· DR. LAURENCE J. PETER ·

. . . And even smarter, how we acquire it by
pretending to be an idiot.

Politeness dictates that, as a guest, we should offer to help with the dishes, and sometimes with meal preparation. However, politeness doesn't dictate that we actually have to do it. This chapter gives us some fun ways to offer help without actually having to do anything. Specifically, we look at the three main tools of holiday-time slackerdom: incompetence, avoidance, and appearance.

Incompetence

One of the greatest tools to get out of doing stuff is incompetence. Either by feigning stupidity, or by actually being gifted as naturally unable to function, you can gain many an hour relaxing on the couch. Think of that bumbling boss who appears incompetent and has her underlings pick up the slack. She's easily smart enough to do all the tasks she dumps onto her subordinates. It's just easier (and smarter) to play stupid. The work still gets done, and she has time for her nail appointment. The same is true of your holiday gathering.

When demonstrating incompetence, it's best to start as soon as possible. On the first day of the visit, "accidentally" break a glass, then "trip" and drop a plate. They'll think you're too clumsy to do anything other than clean up wrapping paper. If you find yourself setting out the silverware for dinner, remember to place the spoon upside down and diagonally. The knife goes with the blade facing the chair, and the fork should be balanced horizontally on the fulcrum of the spoon. They'll either think a poltergeist helped set the table, or that you'd help most by sitting on your hands in front of the TV. If you're being encouraged to wear your mittens indoors, you know that you're masterfully executing the incompetence strategy.

Avoidance

If you've accidentally demonstrated that you are more than capable of helping out, incompetence may not be an option. In this case, you need to work on your avoidance skills. Avoidance is a bit trickier than incompetence, because you must sometimes make risky decisions.

For example, a great way to make sure no one asks you to drive out and pick someone up at the airport is to start drinking the minute you arrive. You fight traffic every day of the year. Today, the only traffic you want to fight is on the way to the bathroom after your seventh beer.

But what if you decide you want to get away from the festivities for a while? Maybe sitting sober in traffic is more fun than being drunk around relatives. To get the drive-out-to-the-airport assignment, you've got to risk being functional (unless your family is cool with drinking and driving—in which case they should hold off setting the table until they know how many place settings they'll need). Now you've got a decision to make: avoid driving to the airport, or spending time with family. This will be a personal judgment call. If you do head out to the airport, be sure to return with just enough time to wash your hands and sit down. You don't want to leave any time that could be used to help set the table. See if whoever you pick up needs to stop by a store, catch a movie, have a drink at a gentlemen's club, etc. Make sure his or her prearrival needs are completely met.

For basic avoidance tactics, the key to success is good timing. For example, immediately after dinner, excuse yourself to the bathroom. Don't return until you know that volunteers have already been selected for dishwashing and the majority of the work is already done. Then walk back to the kitchen and quickly ask, "Do you want me to help with the dishes?" They'll think you mean to help them clean off the leftover mashed-potato slurry and roast-beef grease, but that you just have bad timing.

APPEARANCE

The final weapon in our arsenal of inactivity is making it appear as though we are doing chores. When people are setting the table, pick up a single spoon and polish it furiously. Let everyone see how hard you're working to make sure that whoever gets that spoon will have a spot-free soup experience. It will appear as though you've been an equal participant in the dinner preparation party, even if all you did was pretend to polish an already spotless spoon. Another important part of maintaining the appearance of assistance is to talk about doing chores. Incorporate chore-doing into your stories: "So I'm doing the dishes, right? Just scrubbing several dishes and rinsing glasses, when all of a sudden, a sasquatch ran across your backyard deck. I was so shocked, I had to pause a moment before continuing to scrub the pots and pans." A story like this can leave no doubt that you're pulling your weight.

TAKE A LOAD OFF, SALLY

Take these tactics, go have a seat in your favorite chair, and enjoy the festivities. If you get thirsty, ask someone to bring you a soda. I'm sure they won't mind helping you out. And lest you feel the slightest bit of guilt, remember that it's your time as much as theirs. You want to enjoy your family this holiday, not wait on them.

SURVIVAL TIPS

1. When in doubt about which tactic to use, go with incompetence. People can't get angry at an idiot.

2. Being polite is different than being helpful. Just ask any Home Depot employee.

chapter 11

BOOZING UP BABY (AND PUPPY)
(HOW TO GIVE ALCOHOL TO CHILDREN OR DOGS AS A WAY TO SPRUCE UP THE EVENING'S ENTERTAINMENT—AND NOT GET IN TROUBLE FOR GIVING ALCOHOL TO CHILDREN OR DOGS)

On the first day of Christmas, my true love gave to me a partridge in a pear tree.

· DRENNON ·

. . . On the second day of Christmas, my parents gave to me, two Long Island Iced Teas . . . the third day of Christmas was a blur.

Children and dogs are some of the cutest things on earth. This chapter shows how getting them drunk makes them even cuter. There are, of course, some people who find the thought of giving alcohol to children (or dogs) to be disturbing and wrong. With them, we may have to agree to disagree. Everyone knows that adults are more fun to be around when they've been drinking. The same is true of our children and dogs (though cats are angry drunks and should not be given alcohol, no matter how much they promise to "be cool this time"). Don't feel bad about inebriating the youngsters. During the holidays, the legal drinking age is ten (nine if they know how to drive a tractor). You know you're a good parent, and you deserve a break from teaching responsibility for a few days. Besides, kids in Italy drink, like, five glasses of wine per day. Just pretend you're on a European vacation, and recognize what many of our old-country cousins already know: nothing's more festive than watching little, hiccupping Jimmy trying to get to second base with the dog (who may not mind, having also had one too many).

WHY YOU SHOULD GIVE ALCOHOL TO KIDS AND DOGS

Lest you fall prey to the "no booze for babies" propaganda, the following should help you to understand the value of partying up with the young'uns.

Kids

- As at any party, we don't want a bunch of sober squares killing the buzz. If we're going to be drinking, we want everyone drinking. We don't want some sober nine-year-old sitting there and judging us.
- Kids can occasionally be shy around adults. Nothing cures shyness like a little liquid courage. They'll go from blushing when you ask how school's going to demanding that the entire family go to Denny's for some bacon and eggs.
- The increasing demands of our jobs means that there are fewer opportunities to do things as a family. We all know the power of bonding with co-workers and friends over some brews. Let's do

the same with our kids. If your ten-year-old wakes up, looks at you, and asks, "Dude, what did we do last night?" you'll have a family memory the kid can take with him for the rest of his life (even if the memory is just of his first blackout).

■ Kids sometimes have a hard time talking to their cousins or other rarely seen family members. A little bit of alcohol can give your kid the courage to walk up and ask, "So, what are you into, like SpongeBob or something? Me, I'm more of a Wiggles kid, but I can see the artistic value of a talking sponge. Hey, you wanna get out of here? I know an anthill in the backyard we can pour gasoline into."

■ Kids always want to feel more grown up. After a few drinks, they won't be able to tell if they're at the kids' table—or under it.

Dogs

■ Dogs are perhaps the family members most in need of our approval. Why not let them finally feel like part of the "cool crowd" by pouring them a cold one?

■ If you've grown tired of the holiday conversation, watching sure-footed Rex trying to walk a straight line is a lot of fun. It's like an episode of *Cops*, except it's not weird that your dog isn't wearing a shirt.

■ Give your dog the gift of a good excuse for peeing in the house. No one has ever hit you in the head with a newspaper for committing a party foul.

■ There are television shows built around dogs doing dumb things. Nothing ensures doing dumb things more than alcohol. Get the video camera and prepare to win a free T-shirt.

■ There's a limit to how many years you can stick fake reindeer antlers on your dog and think it's fun. This year, see how cute it is when your dog thinks your grandfather's prosthetic leg is a tree.

HOW DARE YOU—SHE'S JUST A CHILD

Like mentioned above, there are some family members who don't
think kids (or dogs) should drink. Out of respect for their misguided
beliefs, we need a few ways to disguise our giving alcohol to kids and
dogs; or ways to convince them that we aren't getting them drunk.
We're just letting them taste our wine (every five minutes).

■ *Vodka means water in Russian:* Have you ever been in a city where
   the tap water tastes "funny"? This holiday, give that uptight
   nephew or anxious niece a glass of water that not only tastes
   funny, but makes them *feel* funny. Vodka is the ideal spirit to help
   those kids loosen up and have a good time. Tell them it's a special
   tap water that only comes to the faucet this time of year, and only
   to boys and girls who've been good (mean boys and girls have to
   drink tequila). Of course, let them know that, during this holiday, it
   is not recommended that you drink eight glasses of water per day.
■ *Open a present, do a shot:* Every family has its traditions. Some
   open presents the night before, whereas others go to church.
   Why not start your own tradition that combines a drinking
   game with the unwrapping of presents? The best part is, it won't
   matter what presents you buy the others; they'll probably tell
   you that they love you anyway (or pick a fight if they're angry
   drunks).
■ *Beer in the toilet:* If you're worried about someone's giving you a
   hard time for pouring beer into the dog's water dish, just pour
   some beer into the toilet and let the dog have a drink. You'll
   notice that the dog has found his treat when he ambles back into
   the living room like a college freshman stumbling down fraternity row.
■ *Accidentally spill your beer:* This is a double gift for the little pooch.
   Dogs live for spilled food and drink. This time, the treat won't

just taste good going down, but a few minutes later, your golden retriever can delight the party with his Nick Nolte impression.

12 OUNCES OF CUTENESS

If there's ever a lull in the festivities, remember that nothing brings back the merriment like our precious ones falling all over themselves. Dogs want to do anything human, even if that means making an ass of themselves and then waking up with a headache. And kids typically go from cranky to happy to sleepy to psychotic during the holidays. Now, they can have the same excuse adults do for their mood swings.

SURVIVAL TIPS

1. Some people say that giving alcohol to kids can hurt their mental development. Yeah, if they're trying to develop into wallflowers.

2. Please don't really give your kids booze (unless they have trouble sleeping, or they're nervous before a big soccer game).

3. Giving your dog booze is an act of mercy. Think about it: how many bows could you bear being stuck on your head while everyone around you laughs, before you'd need a drink?

IV

IF YOU'RE WATCHING THIS VIDEO, IT MEANS I'M DEAD AND YOU'VE JUST TURNED THIRTEEN

(SURVIVING BAR MITZVAHS, GRADUATIONS, AND BIRTHDAYS)

chapter 12

THE EXCUSE WILL SET YOU FREE
(HOW TO GET OUT OF ATTENDING A BAR MITZVAH, GRADUATION, OR BIRTHDAY)

He that is good for making excuses is
seldom good for anything else.

· BENJAMIN FRANKLIN ·

. . . Yeah, but if you're really good at making
excuses, you don't have to do anything else.

Sometimes, you just can't make it to a bar mitzvah, graduation, or birthday. It's not your fault. You just found out that the Oxygen Channel is running Oprah's five favorite episodes from the past year. You can't miss watching them. It'd be like telling Oprah you don't love her. Nephews graduate from medical school all the time, but five straight hours of Oprah is a not-to-be-missed event.

It's clear that the right thing to do is come up with a good excuse for why you won't be at the graduation, grab a drum of ice cream, and spend the day learning how to lose weight, fix your relationship, marvel at single moms who've become millionaires, and know what books you should read so as to not feel guilty for spending an entire day watching TV.

wHAT'S A GOOD EXCUSE?

A good excuse must be so absurd and unique that it's unverifiable. If you just tell someone that you can't make his birthday party because you've got the flu or jury duty, it'll sound too reasonable and he'll think you're lying. Your excuse must be farfetched enough for people to think, "There's no way she would've made that up. It must be true." The following are some examples of good excuses that you're free to use or adapt to your own circumstances:

"Hi, I won't be able to make Barbara's birthday party. I got trapped in a sensory-deprivation chamber and can't tell where (or who) I am."

Why it's a good excuse: When was the last time you heard the old "got stuck in a sensory-deprivation chamber" excuse? Compared to telling someone you've got car trouble, it sounds a lot more believable if you tell someone you've misplaced the boundaries to your physical body.

"Hi, I'm not going to be able to make it to Mark's bar mitzvah. I shattered a testicle sliding down a banister. Hearing someone say, 'Today, I am a man,' will be too much to bear."

Why it's a good excuse: It's an injury that can't be verified. Whenever using an injury excuse, choose such things as hernias, debilitating yeast infections, or internal parasites, so you won't have to show your work.

"Hi, I'm not going to be able to make Aunt Gilda's seventieth birthday bash. I'm being held hostage in Tehran."

Why it's a good excuse: You've clearly used the one phone call the Iranian government gave you to tell them you won't be able to make it. You could've called the embassy or a human rights group. But your only concern before having to say, "Death to America," live on Al Jazeera is that your auntie knows that you're sorry for missing her party.

"Hi, I'm not going to be able to make it to Lisa's birthday party. I woke up in a bathtub full of ice with a kidney missing."

Why it's a good excuse: While this is a famous urban legend, it could happen. Who can think about cake and balloons when you've got a note taped to your forehead that reads, "Call 911 or you'll die!"?

"Hi, I won't be able to make it to Santosh's graduation. I accidentally sent an e-mail threatening to kill the president, and now I'm under house arrest."

Why it's a good excuse: None of your relatives will want to associate with a known criminal, especially one who might tune the feds into the fact that Aunt Sharon failed to report last year's garage-sale earnings.

"I won't be able to make it to Mindy's bat mitzvah. Some Japanese businessmen showed up at my house and demanded that I take them out to get drunk."

Why it's a good excuse: Everyone knows that if Japanese business-men knock on your door, not taking them out to get plastered is considered an insult. Of course, the relative might say, "Get them drunk at the bat mitzvah." So be prepared to respond with, "Are there going to be strippers there? That was also part of the deal." (Note: While strippers are considered offensive in America, in Japan they are revered as "honorable woman who lip-syncs Madonna songs for rent money.")

BUT PLEASE TELL THEM I SAID CONGRATULATIONS

Keep in mind that most people don't even care if you show up for their bar mitzvahs, graduations, or birthdays. Most kids just want presents. For you to hang out at a kid's party is like the FedEx driver hanging around after he's delivered a package. Just sign the card and be on your way. And relatives celebrating their eightieth- or nine-tieth-birthday party won't even remember if you've attended. So if you've got a once-in-a-lifetime opportunity to attend a boat show or take an all-day nap, do the right thing. Tell your loved one you can't make it to her party because you've fallen down a well. She'll completely understand.

SURVIVAL TIPS

1. Sometimes, as much as you'd like to waste a Saturday at some relatives' "all about us" fest, you've got more important things to do, like sitting on the couch while contemplating which set of Tony Robbins's CDs will get you rich the quickest.

2. Respect excuses for the role they play in society. If employees hadn't learned to say, "I went to a rock concert over the weekend," there would be mass firings from failed drug tests.

3. Add the phrase "This is going to sound made up" at the beginning of every excuse. This way, she'll think, "There's no way he would've made up this excuse *and* practically admitted it. It must be legit."

chapter 13

HOW TO GIVE A GIFT THAT PUTS THE ATTENTION BACK ON YOU

Carpe diem.

· SOME ROMAN ·

. . . I think that means seize their day.

Have you ever shown up to some celebration, only to learn that it's entirely focused on some relative who isn't you? How painful is it to arrive and see that the cake only has one name on it—and it's not yours? It can ruin your entire party!

What can you do? If you turn around and leave, other people might mistake your behavior for a selfish temper tantrum. You could arrive with an extra piping-bag of frosting and add your name to the cake, but if they weren't thoughtful enough to think of you when they ordered it, there's no reason to fix their mistake now.

These people leave us no choice but to turn his party into ours, make a grand entrance, or give a gift that may not be what that person wanted, but will no doubt remind everyone else at the party that you're there as well.

THROWING A SURPRISE PARTY

Your family is so distracted by your sister's graduation from medical school that they've forgotten you even exist. To help them remember, you're going to throw a surprise party. Unlike a surprise party in the olden days, where the guest of honor is ambushed by all her guests, a bunch of guests will now suddenly realize they've ended up at *your* party.

RIDE A HORSE, SAVE A BIRTHDAY

The most important part of a successful surprise party is to make an entrance. And nothing does this better than arriving fashionably late upon a trusty steed. You can rent a horse almost anywhere these days (you can even Priceline them in some cities). Don't park the horse outside—just ride her into the bar mitzvah, birthday, or graduation. Gallop proudly into the event, and make sure to have some trumpeters announcing your arrival (you'd be surprised what a high school marching band will do for some extra cash).

This brings us to the first "gift." Dismount the horse and tell the guest of honor that your gift to her is a trail ride. Urge her to leave the party and go for a trot immediately, since the horse has to be back by three P.M. or they'll charge your credit card for an extra day. Once she rides out, you'll have successfully dispatched your rival. Then stand on a chair and say, "I have an announcement, everyone. I was recently promoted to Roving Balloon Animal Maker at the volunteer circus!" Since you're now the only one around with something to celebrate, all your relatives will have nothing to do but congratulate you on your accomplishment. It's as though they've been at your party all along. Surprise!

OTHER GOOD GIFTS

Although riding in on a horse (the higher the horse you ride in on the better) is a great way to surprise your relatives, there are some other great gifts that will help them recognize what a great and thoughtful person you are:

- *Emus:* Nothing turns heads like a big, beautiful, flightless bird. Of course, no one likes to wait for a gift, so show up with emu in hand (but better to have it on a leash and in shackles). If the gift is for a guy's fiftieth-birthday bash, you can even have the emu jump out of a cake.

- *A beehive:* They say bees are disappearing from the ecosystem, so what better gift to give than a rare, valuable swarm of bees? Nothing will make an octogenarian's day more than watching a member of his family trot in on a horse, in full beekeeping gear, while tossing around a beehive as though it were a football. People will probably run out into the street, unable to contain their excitement.

- *An organ-meat gift basket:* If you're looking for a more modest gift for your favorite carnivore, nothing says, "I dare you to eat this," like a selection of fine organ meats from the waste bucket of your local butcher. It's a gift that comes right from the heart (as well as the lungs and pancreas).

- *A lifetime supply of toothpaste:* There's no better gift for a bar mitzvah boy who's hitting the age at which he may be self-conscious about his breath than five pallets of his favorite plaque-fighting paste delivered right to the dance floor. It may send him scurrying to the corner to check his breath. But while he's breathing into his hand and wondering if he'll ever kiss a girl, you're free to bask in the admiration of your relatives. It's recommended that you walk around with your arms open, in case anyone wants to hug you.

No, Really, You Didn't Have To

Our relatives don't mean to overlook us when they plan some nephew's college graduation party, or our dad's fiftieth-birthday bash. They're just so absorbed in their own selfish desire to honor someone else, they forget about us. With the suggestions in this chapter, you should rest easy knowing that no matter whose celebration you're invited to, you will always be the *real* guest of honor.

Survival Tips

1. Always ride a horse to someone's celebration. If you absolutely cannot find a horse, then donkeys, ponies, and goats may also work. Just be sure they can support your weight. If your great-grandfather can't go three feet without his walker, showing up on an animal that can barely move won't lift his spirits.

2. When bringing an emu for a lucky bar mitzvah boy, it's okay to bring it into a synagogue—so long as it's wearing a yarmulke.

3. Above all, remember that your family loves you. Even if they say this party is for someone else, with a small reminder (like arriving with a box of hissing cockroaches), all they'll be able to think about is you.

PART

V

YOU CAN NEVER GO HOME AGAIN
(BUT YOU CAN MOVE BACK IN WITH YOUR PARENTS)

chapter 14

RE-ENTRY STRATEGY

My parents have been really supportive
right from the very beginning.

· BENJAMIN COHEN ·

. . . Then what's a few more years going to hurt?

If you plan on moving back in with your parents, it's actually a sign
of a bright future (unless they've passed away—then it's a sign of
mental illness). How can you start a lucrative slam-poetry career, or
build a ventriloquist act that's sure to make you the talk of the town,
if you're busy working? Paying rent and feeding oneself is creatively
stifling. The way to realize your childhood dreams of leisure and
wealth is to return to the place where you were a child.

FIRST CONTACT (AGAIN)

Your parents have probably anticipated that you'll ask to move back
home. Changing your major four times while in college, graduat-
ing on the seven-year plan, then getting fired from three jobs in six

months was a signal that you're obviously too talented and creative to be among the general public. Soon, you'll return home to launch your Bill Gates–like empire.

Even though your parents can tell that you're obviously made for something more than paying your bills, when you return home you shouldn't tell them what your true intentions are. You know in your heart that you're only a year of piano lessons away from being the next Billy Joel. You know that your idea for a car that runs on Pop Rocks is revolutionary. But your parents may not have your vision and foresight. You're better off telling them how you're going to get a job as that person who offers free food samples at the grocery store until you can convince a company that despite having a degree in English (and the ability to speak it perfectly), you're still qualified to work in technical support.

Your Room or Their Den?

When you moved out of the house, your parents were so distraught by your absence that they quickly filled your room with sewing machines, yoga balls, and knife collections, just to dull the pain of your absence. Now that you're moving back in, it will almost be too much joy for them to handle. In fact, the minute you move in, they may start asking if you've found a job yet, just so they don't get their hopes up that your stay will be permanent.

That's why you must be careful while moving back into your room. At first, just occupy the bed. Don't move their stuff into the basement. If you move too fast, they're liable to tell you that you're disrupting their lives and you've got six months to find your own place. Don't take this seriously. It's just a defense mechanism against feeling the heartbreak they experienced the first time you left (in fact, the minute you were gone, they probably went on a Hawaiian vacation to escape their misery). Wait at least a month. Then, after you think your parents are comfortable with your presence, trip over your mom's yoga ball and accidentally stab yourself with one of your father's antique daggers. They'll be so concerned for your safety (or that you've got no health insurance) that they'll help you move their stuff. Then give it another month before rehanging your Metallica posters.

WHAT'S FOR DINNER, MOM?

To build your home-based business based on the DVDs you ordered from an infomercial (if that guy sitting on a yacht can become rich, so can you!), you're going to need a healthy diet. Who better to feed the mind that's about to get rich buying homes with no money down, than your own mom? And don't feel bad about asking her to cook all your meals. Britney Spears has a personal chef, so why shouldn't you?

The easiest mom to get cooking is a guilty mom. She loves you and wants nothing more than to make up for the fact that when you were a child, she put her aerobics schedule ahead of her parenting. Your being home is a chance to be the mother that her body dysmorphia never let her be.

The toughest mom to get in the kitchen is the one who believes that she retired from cooking the day you left. She's probably beside herself (with happiness) that you're back at home, and doesn't want to risk disappointing you with her atrophied cooking skills.

For this kind of mom, you should begin by asking her if she needs anything from the store. She'll probably say no, but keep asking and soon she'll begin to feel like she must reciprocate and ask if *you* want anything from the store. Have your list ready, so it's easy for her. As you hand her the list, ask, "Oh, can you pick up stuff to make lasagna? You make the best lasagna. Remember when I was a kid and

you'd make it for me?" This is the kind of coaxing and encourage-
ment she'll need to get back in the kitchen on your behalf.

THREE TO FIVE WITH GOOD BEHAVIOR

Now that you've settled into your room and have a ready supply of
meals, let's focus on how to not wear out your welcome. Even though
your parents are thrilled to have you home, they're probably worried
that their advancing age may not allow them to take care of you the
way they'd like to. In fact, they may be so scared of letting you down
that they'll constantly ask when you're going to get that job you keep
talking about. To put your parents at ease, about once a week, you
should say, "Remember, you guys, this arrangement is temporary. I
was *this* close to getting that job as a Secret Service agent, but then
I told someone about the interview and it blew my cover." Telling
them that your stay is temporary should be part of your weekly
maintenance plan.

WOW, DAD! I HAD NO IDEA YOU COULD MAKE NAPALM FROM GASOLINE AND STYROFOAM

Chances are, your dad will be the one who most eagerly wants you
out of the house. While he's as happy that you're home as the day he
found out your mother was pregnant, your presence is cutting into his
walking-around-naked time. He's had to spend years making sure the
kids were asleep before pulling out the leather masks and love oil. It
will threaten the duration of your stay if he begins to see you as the
prodigal cock-blocker. To make sure he doesn't resent your presence
to the point that he packs your bags while you're down at the music
store "networking" with the assistant manager, prepare to pucker up.

Smile and absorb all the tales no one else wants to hear from him. Pretend to be interested in his golf stories, feign fascination when he spends three hours describing the inner workings of an integrated circuit, and when he rails about the government, support him as though things would be done right if, dammit!, only he were in power. If all else fails, ask him if he's started growing more hair. Even if he's bald as an electrode-covered lab rat, it'll buy you at least a year.

DID YOU THROW OUT MY BASEBALL CARDS?

Despite all your guile and strategy, you're actually doing your parents a favor by moving back home. Not only are you adding some sunshine to their golden years, but you're also about to build a business that will make your entire family wealthy beyond belief—just as soon as you watch one more episode of *South Park*.

SURVIVAL TIPS

1. Your mother will be your greatest ally in helping you to stay as long as you like. Even the most dysfunctional mother loves her child. Even if she shows her love by asking if you want to join her cannabis club.

2. If your parents ask you to live in the basement when you arrive, do as they request. They'll let you have your own room back as soon as they realize how hard it is to sleep above the sound of someone practicing bowling-pin juggling.

3. Don't be in any rush to move out. It will take at least three years to go from learning how to turn on your Casio keyboard to becoming a Grammy Award–winning musician.

chapter 15

IN MY HOUSE, YOU'LL LIVE BY MY RULES
(AND ONE OF THOSE RULES IS THAT YOU CAN'T LIVE IN MY HOUSE)

Generosity gives assistance, rather than advice.

· MARQUIS DE VAUVENARGUES ·

. . . So don't advise your kid to find an apartment.
Assist him in packing his bags.

As a parent, it was your dream, once the kids moved out, to finally install that sex swing and start going at it so crazily that should a young child happen to walk in, he'd wonder if you were making a baby, or making an innocent person confess to a crime. But now one of your offspring has sprung back into your house, and you can't have any fun. He's killing your buzz, man.

It's not that you don't want to help your kid out. In fact, you're part of the reason his twenty-six-year-old ass is indenting your couch. If you'd played a more active role in his life, maybe he would've gotten an engineering degree instead of studying musical theater in the hope that an audience's love might fill the void created when you opted to bring the dog instead of him to the father-son picnic. Even though you explained that to win the relay race you needed a partner who doesn't have asthma, he still didn't understand.

However, there comes a point when Junior must fend for himself. You may not have been the best parent. But you didn't beat him, and you paid for his college. You've earned your parole.

HAPPY BIRTHDAY—I BOUGHT YOU A NEW SUITCASE

It's in your best interests to be gentle during the kid removal process. Ideally, you want him to leave of his own accord, rather than being directly asked to pack up. When you're older, you'll need someone who can tend to your yard, take you shopping, and help you cruise for widows at the retirement village. Of all your kids, this "late bloomer" is probably the one who'll have the time to help. If you hurt his feelings, he may become independent and successful just to spite you. Then, who'll mow your lawn?

And there's always a chance that your crackpot kid might actually come through on one of his inventions. He'll be rich, but your harsh shove from the nest will eliminate any chance of him buying you that tricked out, rocket-powered Rascal scooter. You'll be confined to the 3 mph red supermarket version, like all the other suckers.

Let's take a look at how to get your house back without having to change the locks:

MY ROOMMATES THINK THEY OWN THE PLACE

One of the perceived benefits of living at home, as far as your kid's concerned, is that he doesn't have to deal with roommates. Out in the real world, there are energy bills to dicker about, cleaning responsibilities to negotiate, and red rags to tie on doorknobs, indicating that someone has "company." Typically, roommates are disgusting people who eat your food, leave things to rot in the refrigerator, play their music while you're sleeping, and get pissed when you play yours.

Well, if it's a bad roommate your kid's trying to escape, it's a bad roommate you'll be. Of course, there are other reasons your kid has decided to reclaim his three-bedroom, two-bath womb. He may not want to work, or he may just not want to grow up. No matter what the reason, your job is to be such a miserable roommate that he'd sooner take up residence in an underground sewer pipe (at least then, no one would accuse him of hogging the bathroom) than spend another night with parents who think that using your "indoor voice" means talking louder because you're safely in the confines of home.

The good news is that this task is made infinitely easier by the fact that parents are naturally repulsive to their offspring. What do you think a kid will find more gruesome: some stranger walking around in his underwear while using his fingers to scoop peanut butter from a jar, or his own mother or father doing that? A parent's gross-out factor is much higher. You must use this to your advantage.

Therefore, when you've decided it's time for your kid to take that money he's been saving for an airbrush and use it to put up first and last month's rent, don't push him out of the nest—just leave your underwear hanging in the bathroom.

DUDE, THAT BURRITO CLEARLY HAD MY NAME ON IT

It's highly unlikely that your freeloading kid will actually buy or bring home his own food. But if he ever does, you must eat it. If he questions you about it, say, "Dude, I didn't eat your food. Maybe you ate it when you were high." If he tries to retaliate and eat your leftovers, be sure to booby-trap them by leaving a set of false teeth clenched into the burger or floating in the wonton soup. If you don't have a set of falsies lying around, leaving a dirty fork or spoon in the dish will also work.

Make sure to keep your fridge stocked with food so rotten and moldy that it's two days away from morphing into an organism. If you have to, go Dumpster-diving to stock up on past-due foodstuffs. Should you see a dead squirrel on the road, put it in a Styrofoam container and write "enchiladas—do not eat!" on the lid. Your kid won't be able to resist violating the "do not eat" edict. When he opens the container to find road kill, he'll realize that even if he were to share an apartment with that guy who raps to himself at the bus stop, it might be better than another week with his parents.

CLOTHES

Borrowing someone's clothes is a step below borrowing someone's toothbrush. Provided that you're within a few weight classes of the youngster, make sure that, every Saturday morning, he wakes up to find you eating an omelet in his oversized "Tupac Lives" T-shirt. When he asks, "Why are you wearing my shirt?" just say, "I'm representing." If he follows with, "Yeah? What the hell are you representing?" say, "I'm representing parents everywhere who are sick of their twenty-six-year-old kids leaving clothes in the dryer."

Is This The Position We Used To Conceive Junior?

Most people would rather watch their own heart surgery than catch a glimpse of their parents having sex (at least then, if you hear "oh God," it's because you've suddenly started approaching a white light). If messing with your kid's food and wearing his clothes hasn't inspired him to move out, then it's time for the heavy artillery. It's time for him to catch you and his mother knocking boots.

Begin by nonchalantly asking your kid to run to the store and pick up some butter. The minute he leaves, get to it in the family room. He'll return to find two middle-aged masses of flesh voiding the warranty on the loveseat. Nothing makes a kid want to get on with his life more than seeing his folks doing it. Once you've registered the horror in his eyes, start giggling and scuttle back to the bedroom. Before you shut the door, turn to your kid and say, "Son, I'll take that butter now."

And when you reappear an hour later, make sure the only thing you have on is his Tupac shirt.

Your Mother And I Will Miss You

Remember, this isn't just about getting to live out your golden years in peace. Becoming the roommate from hell will also help your child get on with his life. Even if you just employ one of the above tactics, your kid will be painting his new studio apartment sooner than you can say, "Honey, do you remember where I left the Benoit Balls?"

SURVIVAL TIPS

1. Seeing parents have sex is like looking through a high-powered telescope to see the beginning of the universe, except that it's totally gross.

2. If you're disturbed by the thought of using sex as an eviction tactic, just think of it like you're the bad guy in an episode of *Scooby-Doo*. You can't tell your kid to leave, but you can scare him away by putting on a mask and filling the hallway with the sounds of moans and shrieks.

3. If your kid ever gets angry at you for wearing his clothes, just tell him that he's welcome to wear something of yours—then throw him a Depends.

PART

VI

PuBerty, MenoPause, and Other Excuses For Being a Pain in the Ass

chapter 16

YOU DON'T UNDERSTAND, MOM!
(PUBERTY AND ADOLESCENCE)

Puberty was very vague. I literally locked myself
in a room and played guitar.

· JOHNNY DEPP ·

. . . Yeah, I'm sure that's what you were playing.
Just be thankful you weren't rehearsing for
Edward Scissorhands.

To survive a family member stricken with puberty, you must be very brave. It can be uncomfortable to notice your kids beginning to mature sexually. He used to love it when you'd read to him. Now the only bedtime stories he wants to hear involve being asked to stay after class by his English teacher, Mrs. Robinson. This can be a very tough time for both parent and adolescent. Whatever you do, don't ignore that little hypothalamus gland running around your house. He or she needs your support in three crucial areas: teenage pregnancy, drugs, and gangs.

Let's talk about Sex, baby

Nothing can make a mess of your social calendar like becoming a grandmother before you're forty. Not to mention how tough it will be on your daughter, who must now find a date to the senior ball who's willing to buy her a corsage *and* hire a babysitter.

To make sure this doesn't happen, you've got to attack the problem where it starts: at the hormonal level. Our bodies mature as though the average lifespan is still thirty and we'd better give birth to as many kids as possible before getting trampled by rhinos. It was once considered natural to have kids at seventeen. Today, it either means that you've made a mistake or you're Amish.

The way to combat this is to create a psychological barricade between arousal and action. To do this, take your kid on a field trip to the local free clinic. Bring a porno flick and a DVD player. Have a seat in the waiting room, and start showing the dirty movie. As you notice the eyes bulging out of your youngster's head, point to a strung-out, baggy-eyed, nineteen-year-old mother of two who's pushing one in a stroller while shouting at the other from across the room: "Billy, give Mommy her lighter back and sit down!" Tell your child, "See? That's what happens when you do those things in the movie!" If you have a starter's pistol or air horn, you can also jar your kid with a loud noise to further connect arousal to discomfort.

You don't have to limit the negative conditioning to teenage mothers. Even if you see a guy with a broken arm, you can point to the porno and say, "That guy broke his arm because he had sex." Then hit the air horn.

With this helpful conditioning, your little one should have no problem making it through his or her teenage years without conceiving. Sure, your kid may have some "issues" to work out later in life. (Should she have kids of her own one day, and her daughter returns from a soccer game with a sprained ankle, she'll ask, "Who've you been messing around with?") But what issues would you rather deal with if the shoe were on the other foot: explaining why you feel that you need health insurance to have an orgasm, or why, despite your aspirations to go to college, you've decided it'd be more fun to spend your life as the woman on a road-construction crew who holds the "slow" sign.

Lucy In The Basement With Cubic Zirconium

Drugs are very bad for a developing human (unless that human is trying to develop into a pop star or child actress). Our biggest concern isn't that they try a bit of marijuana, it's that they get so stoned, they forget to graduate high school and pursue their dreams of no longer being a financial burden. To make sure your kid understands what drugs can do to his life, you're going to use a negative conditioning technique similar to the one used to ward off teenage pregnancy. You're going to tell him he can try anything he wants, but he's got to do it with the other toker in the family: forty-three-year-old Uncle Inappropriate, who still lives in his parents' basement. Your kid can get blasted, but only while listening to his weird uncle brag that the drive-thru girl at Burger King likes him, based on the number of extra onion rings he finds at the bottom of the bag. If he wants to see how much fun "using" is, he can do it while attempting to decline his uncle's offer to show him his "magazine" stash. Now, when someone asks if he wants to get high, all he'll be able to think about is his creepy uncle trying to convince him that he wrote the lyrics to Billy Joel's "Captain Jack."

BLOODS, CRIPS, AND THE COHENS

Getting mixed up with gangs is probably one of the most danger-ous things a youngster can do. Fortunately, it's also easy to prevent. A kid joins a gang if he (a) needs protection from other kids who want to kick his ass, or (b) doesn't feel like he belongs to anything worthwhile. To satisfy both of these needs, show your kid that he's already in a gang: your family. This involves actually turning your family into a posse. Choose a nice color (whatever goes with your wallpaper will probably be fine) and then choose some turf to defend. Typically, your turf should be your home address, but if you've got a cabin somewhere, or a timeshare, that's also your turf. If a rival gang (like the neighbors) steps across 223 Elm Street, let it be known you will straight call Brinks Home Security on their asses. For an added touch, give your family members gang names, like "Cleenz His Room" or "Bathroom Hawg." Your kid will swell with pride to be part of the family gang. He might even get a tattoo of Grandma on his elbow (where the wrinkles will add some realism).

A NOTE ABOUT REBELLION

There will come a time when your child decides that the right thing to do is whatever you don't want her to. She'll try to be the complete opposite of you in every way. So make sure you're the opposite of whatever you don't want her to be. That may mean throwing on some black nail polish and fishnet stockings, and blaring some Green Day or Nine Inch Nails. It may mean that, instead of saying grace before each meal, you have your family shut their eyes, lower their heads, and say, "Screw society! Those conformist pigs crush our freedoms. We only eat this food so we have enough energy to fight the Man!"

Your kid will be upstairs doing her homework before you can ask if she'd like to contact Che Guevara through a séance.

WHY'S THE WATER RUNNING IN THE BATHROOM?

Our son or daughter's puberty can be quite easy to survive if we prepare to help them with the challenges they face. So long as we keep them from getting pregnant, becoming junkies, or joining a gang, they can go on to live normal lives—as workaholics and codependents.

SURVIVAL TIPS

1. Turn your family into a gang. Just make sure the CIA doesn't try to get you hooked on crack cocaine.

2. The famous "I have a headache" excuse actually came from mothers showing their daughters provocative pictures, then hitting them in the head to disrupt their fantasies. It was a primitive yet effective form of birth control.

3. Mothers play a big role in shaping their daughters' ideas of being women. As such, try to avoid working at Hooters while your child's an adolescent. This tells her that she isn't becoming a woman, she's becoming a waitress. Also, lay off the Brazilian waxings for a few years. It's tough enough for a girl to accept her bushy new body hair without wondering why Mommy's is trimmed into the shape of Boeing Field.

chapter 17
WHAT'S GOT YOU ALL HOT?
(SURVIVING AND SUPPORTING THE MENOPAUSAL)

Women know when they've got
the menopause, but men don't quite know.
They know it afterwards.

· OMAR SHARIF ·

. . . Yeah, they know it after they get called
bastards for leaving a light on and heating up
the house.

There are plenty of books on how to survive menopause from the sufferer's point of view. What about those of us who must spend time with these beloved, internally combusting matriarchs? How are *we* to survive their change of life? To begin with, let's see what our wives, sisters, and siblings are up against.

WHAT IS MENOPAUSE?

Just as lepers were once quarantined to islands before science revealed that leprosy isn't highly communicable, so should we learn a bit about menopause to clear up any notion that it's a punishment from God, and start shipping women off to colonies (although they may form naturally in the frozen-foods aisle of the supermarket). Let's review some of the basics:

What is menopause?

Menopause is when a woman stops ovulating so she can take up her new hobby of sweating and being grouchy. It's caused by a drop in female hormones. It's also caused by having been called "Mom" 217,000 times. After a while, your body starts to fight back.

What are the symptoms of menopause?

Most notably, the woman's husband becomes an asshole. That's typically the first sign. Then she may have vaginal dryness, which she'll attribute to her lack of desire to have sex with said husband. But all that moisture has to go somewhere, so the woman typically begins to have night sweats. Women enjoy sweating so much that they usually stay up night after night to do it (also called insomnia). And if that isn't enough, during the day, some women have hot flashes.

What are hot flashes?

Hot flashes are when a woman's secret desire to be a shopping-mall Santa Claus shows itself. Years of frustration at having to play an elf or the diminutive Mrs. Claus rear up in a set of hot, jolly cheeks. If you ask a menopausal woman why she wants to be Santa Claus, the lapses in memory and inability to focus will prevent her from telling you.

When does menopause occur?

Menopause typically hits women between the ages of forty-six and fifty-four. However, it can come earlier or later, depending on how many electrical towers are near your home.

Is menopause an illness (you know, like homosexuality)?

No. While menopause can make women, and the men around them, feel sick, menopause is a healthy, natural part of life. Unfortunately, it's the healthy, natural part of life we wish didn't happen.

PLEASE CALL NOW AND GIVE YOUR SUPPORT

It's easy to see how menopause can make a person's life quite miserable. If a wild animal were in that much pain, we'd put it out of its misery. But our dear mothers, sisters, and wives deserve better. They deserve our kindness, understanding, and support. Who you are in relation to her will affect exactly how you should do this:

- *Husbands:* You may feel that having a menopausal wife is like being married to a hangover. Try to be more considerate and make sure you're there for her needs during this tough time. If you need to, join a support group. Find one in which you can talk, listen, get beers, watch sports, go to wet T-shirt contests, and so on, as many nights a week as you need to. If your wife asks why you're gone all the time, tell her you've joined a support group so you can be there for her.
- *Children:* As children, respect how special you will now appear to your mother. She's no longer making eggs, and may look upon you as though you are the last relic of a discontinued china pattern. To comfort your menopausal mother, make goo-goo and

gaga sounds—you can even go shopping with her and throw a fit in the checkout line, if you think it will spark the right nostalgia.

■ *Siblings:* If your older sister's going through menopause, please avoid stories about how you bought a carton of eggs that were expired. Don't mention if the water pipes in your house have suddenly frozen up dry as a bone and no amount of massaging or turning knobs can get the moisture back. You may just think you're making small talk, but it may come across as a reminder of her changing body. Instead, use the benefit of her memory loss to remind her of all the fun things you two did as kids. Tell her stories about when you two used to steal peaches from your neighbor's tree in the springtime, the time she French-kissed Sean Thorpe in a bomb shelter, or about the time she borrowed five hundred dollars from you to produce her own music video—but just ended up having a one-night stand with the guy who worked at the camera store, then needed to borrow five hundred dollars more. You know, remind her of the fun stuff.

THE BLESSING OF BITCHINESS

No matter how much love and support you shower onto these dear changelings, there will be times when they'll still lash out. Nature has given menopausal women the gift of misery. It's only fair that as a caring people, they'll want to share this gift with us. The final advice regarding surviving menopausal women is to see them as Mother Nature's conditioning coaches for dealing with misery. Out in the world, people run into angry, demanding bosses, rude clerks, and irate motorists. If they haven't had enough psychopathic behavior directed toward them at home, they may find these things upsetting. But after a guy's been called an asshole because a bird outside wouldn't stop singing, he won't be fazed in the slightest (although, if she's got a gun, the bird will be).

WHO NEEDS ESTROGEN WHEN YOU'VE GOT FAMILY?

Menopausal women aren't the monsters society makes them out to be. They're our family. If we love them and support them, there's a good chance they won't murder us in our sleep. And if all else fails, remember that menopause is temporary; the ability to make a wife, mother, or sibling feel guilty for the hell she put you through—that lasts forever.

SURVIVAL TIPS

1. Even though menopause can be a very tough time, try to see it as a special event. You can even try thinking of menopause as a holiday—like Easter without the eggs.

2. Since we can't lock the menopausal in a room with an *X* painted on the door, we must see their crankiness as a valuable part of *our* lives. We must remember the following rule: Menopausal bitchiness exists to strengthen family members.

3. Always remember that while menopause might just be happening to one person, it's really a family event. Think back to your last holiday or reunion. There was probably someone red-faced from too much rum, someone sweating profusely after chasing the kids around, and someone who was simply bitchy from not having slept in a week. All three of those people equal one menopausal woman.

VII

I WAS IN LABOR FOR FIFTEEN HOURS AND ALL I GET IS A CARD?

(SURVIVING MOTHER'S DAY AND FATHER'S DAY)

chapter 18

ISN'T BEING YOUR CHILD THANKS ENOUGH?

My parents have been there for me,
ever since I was about seven.

· DAVID BECKHAM ·

... That's when they perfected DNA testing.

Most people would be hard pressed to explain why Mother's Day and Father's Day even exist. We've already blessed our parents with our existence. What greater gift is there? Do you think Joseph, father of Jesus, wanted Christmas *and* Father's Day? The birth of his son was enough. Why isn't that good enough for our parents?

The bottom line is that it's *not* good enough, so rather than fight, the best thing is simply to play the game. Let's take a look at how to manage the four main areas of these Hallmark-sponsored mirages: the phone call, the meal, the gift, and the card.

OH, I THOUGHT I GOT THE MACHINE

Despite all we've done for these people, if we aren't careful, they still might try to turn a phone call into a guilt trip. Here's how to avoid that:

1. Don't open your call with, "Hi, how are you?" An open-ended question puts you at high risk of having to listen to your dad tell you about his slipped disk, that his car won't start, or some boring story about a tingling sensation in his left arm. You don't have time for such nonsense. When you call, the first thing you say is, "Happy Father's Day." That way, all he can say is, "Thank you." (Although he'll probably be biting his tongue not to say, "Don't thank me. Thank your mom's fear that she'd never see me again once I left for Vietnam. Without the spread of communism, you wouldn't exist.")

2. Ask what his plans are for the day. You probably already know that your sister, who isn't wise to this whole hoax, drove through the night just to take him to brunch. But ask anyway, just so you can say, "Darn, I wish I could have been there." If he asks what your plans are for the day, be sure to say something like, "I've got to break boulders into rocks with a sledgehammer," or "I'll be digging a thirty-foot trench." Since he expects you to sacrifice this day to him, it isn't wise to mention that you'll spend it eating ice cream and getting massages.

3. Then drop a quick anecdote into the conversation, some fond memory from the past, like, "Remember when you rushed me to the hospital after I came up with a recipe for Windex smoothies?" You two can take a moment and remember how carefully he placed the towels in the car so you wouldn't throw up on his recently shampooed floor mats. He'll appreciate an anecdote like

that, because it shows that, at one time, you relied on him to save your life (even if he had in fact stored the Windex in an empty Hawaiian Punch container—in your toy chest).

4. Finally, make your dismount. Before your mom or dad can ask when you're going to visit, or if you ever plan on repaying the money they loaned you to hire a hypnotist who said he could help cure your sleep apnea, say, "I've got a call coming in on the other line, let me grab this." The immediacy of another call will save you from having to discuss when they'll hear from you again, if you plan on visiting, or what your children's names are.

THE BRADY BRUNCH

If you are going to visit a parent in person, do it right. Take them to brunch. Our parents cooked our meals for years. Brunch allows them to see what food's like when professionals prepare it. It's an opportunity for our parents to notice that when a server brings over some food, she says, "Enjoy your meal," not, "You're probably going to need to add salt, and eat quickly, because I've got Jazzercise in an hour."

- *The wait:* The best measure of a good brunch is the wait. Even if you've made a reservation, it should still take at least two or three hours to get a table. If it's dinnertime when you can finally sit down for the brunch, your parents will know how much you care.
- *Swan ice sculptures:* No brunch is complete without a giant frozen swan, surrounded of course by shrimp cocktail. If you sit down for brunch and the buffet table boasts nothing more than a flower centerpiece, get up and leave. If your parents sit down for any brunch that doesn't feature an ice sculpture of a deer drinking from a chocolate-fondue pond—or at the very least, a spread-

winged goose attempting to soar high above the seafood salad—they'll consider it a major insult.

- *Pianists and harpsichordist:* Conversations are best if you've got to shout over some high school music teacher's attempt to make a few extra bucks. On the bright side, sitting close to the live music can help you get out of a conversation you don't want to have. If your mother asks, "Remember when you were a little girl and I'd use you to help me shoplift eyeliner?" You can say, "What's that? The pianist? You're right. That is the Muzak version of Courtney Love's 'Doll Parts.'"

GIVE A GIFT THAT SAYS, "LOOK WHAT YOU'VE DONE TO ME."

Another good use of Mother's Day and Father's Day is to thank our parents for making our lives "interesting." Forget the typical gifts. The only time you should give your dad a shaving kit is when he's just been released from prison, or if he's about to undergo gender reassignment and has misplaced his estrogen pills (which for most of us means never). Likewise, think carefully about whether your mom really wants the burden of trying to keep another houseplant alive. Unfortunately, a plant isn't like a child—she can't just stick it in daycare.

Here are some gift suggestions that are a bit more thoughtful, and can help our parents develop a little empathy for what it's like to be their child:

- *Headphones:* There's no better gift for a cold, distant, and uncommunicative mom than a top-of-the-line iPod headset. Get the big ones that NBA players wear. If she wants to shut you out, she can do it in state-of-the-art digital sound.

- *Exotic dancer:* For the father who's spent his life disappointed that you're his third daughter instead of his first son, nothing beats sending him a male Strip-O-Gram. For the first fifteen years of your life, he called you Steve, even though your name is Jennifer—and when you refused to answer to Steve, he started calling you "buddy." As the stripper shakes his junk in your ultraconservative father's face, papa may begin to understand what it's like for someone to mix up what sex you are (unless he really is getting a gender reassignment, in which case he'll "thank you for understanding").

- *Barbie dolls:* For the parent who forced you into beauty contests before you were out of diapers, told your teachers you were sick so you could audition for TV commercials, and once grounded you for eating a doughnut, there's no better gift than a Barbie doll. You were naturally shy and bookish—and the closest you came to being "mommy's little model" was developing an eating disorder in college (although you did break the school record for most doughnuts eaten in a single breakfast). Thanks to your generosity, your parents can finally have their very own micro-human replica with which to play dress-up.

CARD STOCK

The final piece in this charade is to give a card. The primary reason we give our parents a card is simply because they expect one. This year, make the card a bit more meaningful. Don't get anything pre-printed. Use this as another opportunity to communicate your feelings toward them. Here are a few good examples:

Dear Mom,
Every time I yell at my kids, I think of you.
Happy Mother's Day,
Britney

Dear Dad,
Thanks for calling my wife a slut. Every time we talk about you it leads to a big fight, and then really hot make-up sex. Your hatred and jealousy is getting me laid.
Happy Father's Day,
Tommy Lee

Dear Mom,
Thanks for not being there for me. If you hadn't forgotten I was alive, I'd have nothing to rap about.
Happy Mother's Day,
Marshall

THE APPLE DOESN'T FALL FAR, BUT IT DEFINITELY FALLS

For now, Mother's Day and Father's Day are realities. Even if you think it's an embarrassment of riches that our parents have *us* and their own "days," you should still make sure that they know you love them. And who knows—if you raise your own kids right, there may come a time when one of these "special" days in May or June rolls around, and you ask them, "Do you know what today is?" and they say, "Yeah. Sunday."

SURVIVAL TIPS

1. It is always preferable to call on Mother's or Father's Day instead of visiting. In fact, Alexander Graham Bell invented the telephone just so he could get out of seeing Ma Bell.

2. To appease our parents, we must treat Mother's Day and Father's Day as though we're making a burnt offering (although, depending on the quality of your mom's cooking, a burnt offering may be nothing new).

3. If you do go out to brunch with your mom, promise yourself ahead of time that you won't snap, no matter how many times she tells you that you look better when you wear more makeup. And do your best not to reply, "Well, maybe you should wear a little less, Mom! Are you having brunch, or paying homage to Marcel Marceau?"

chapter 19

IN MY DAY, WE HONORED OUR PARENTS BY CHOPPING OFF A FINGER

And then it started, like a guilty thing
upon a fearful summons.

· SHAKESPEARE ·

. . . What started? The only guilty thing that's been
summoned is my son who never calls.

What's wrong with kids these days? We give birth to them, feed them only the sweetest cereals, let them watch TV instead of doing their homework, get them all the ADD medication they could ever want, and when they grow up, we'll even babysit *their* kids so they can go look for second husbands and wives. And what's our reward? An all-you-can-eat seafood buffet and some flowers. And it's just as bad for fathers. What does Dad get for sacrificing his life to someone who hates him for not allowing a nose ring? An electronic tie rack and a coffee mug. Because nothing says "thank you" like more crap to sell at your next garage sale.

I ALMOST DIDN'T RECOGNIZE YOUR VOICE, YOU HAVEN'T CALLED IN SO LONG

Don't buy into the nonsense that guilt is a bad thing. It's simply a way to remind someone of how he or she has wronged you. How else will your kids know that, every week they don't call, a part of you dies? Guilt provides them with that information. When applied properly, it can get you the love, attention, and gifts you deserve. If you're the "World's Best Mom" as the apron he got you last year proclaims, don't you think that achievement is worth more than another book of knitting patterns?

FIVE GOOD GUILT TRIPS

In case you're at a loss for what to make your kids feel guilty about, here are a few suggestions:

1. *Dreams:* Maybe you once dreamed of traveling the world. If only you could've somehow earned rewards miles for driving a kid to and from school, you'd have enough for a free flight to Jupiter. Instead of seeing Kuala Lumpur, you spent that money on orthodontists and summer camp. To this day, you can't look at a globe without wondering what life would've been like if you weren't allergic to latex.

2. *Youthful good looks:* You were once the belle of the beach, but when Junior decided to try and shoot out ass-first, you received a C-section scar that marked the end of your bikini days. Let your child know that there was a time when you used to show off your washboard abs. Thanks to him, you've got a slice across your midsection that makes you look like a disgraced samurai warrior.

Now you're condemned to a life of wearing a matronly one-piece. That kid took your sexy!

3. *Freedom of expression:* You used to say whatever came to mind—until your kid called his kindergarten teacher a dickhead. Then you realized there's some other human who plans on repeating everything you say in front of teachers and pastors. Because of your kid's selfish desire to learn a language, you had to spend fifteen years of your life muffling your true voice under a blanket of, "Ah, Sugars" and "Fiddlesticks!"

4. *Freedom of thought:* You used to use your mind to contemplate the meaning of life. But after having a kid, all your mental energy went to convincing him that paper clips aren't candy—and that just because baking soda's in the refrigerator, it doesn't mean you should feed it to pigeons at the park (unless it's the Fourth of July and you've run out of fireworks).

5. *Freedom of enjoyment:* Not that you and your spouse are pervs, but after having a kid, watching an adult movie together entails soundproofing your bedroom and freezing a Benadryl into your kid's Otter Pop.

BEING SORRY MEANS NEVER HAVING TO SAY, "I LOVE YOU"

Now let's look at how to use your guilt.

1. *The call or greeting:* When they call you or arrive at your house this Mother's Day or Father's Day, you must lay the groundwork for the guilt trip. Begin by feigning illness and senility. Should

your son try the "Hi. Happy Father's Day" trick on you (see previous chapter), pause for five seconds and ask, "Dad, is that you? I thought you were dead." Then, when he says, "No, Dad, it's me, your son," don't answer. Just cough for about a minute straight. Once he asks, "Dad, are you okay?" you are ready to extract the attention and gifts a parent deserves.

2. *Linking the guilt to action:* Once you've got his attention, use the guilt trips included in this chapter, or your own personal favorites to let your kid know how much trouble his existence has caused you. At some point, he's likely to answer, "I'm sorry that happened," or "But things are better now, right?" No matter what he says, respond with, "What would really make it better is if you'd quit your job and visit for the summer." This will most likely be impossible, but at the very least, it'll provoke him to ask, "I can't quit my job, but how about I come out for a week this summer?" Then reply, "Just one week? I spend eighteen years of my life giving you a place to live, and that's only worth a week's visit to you? Why don't you wait and schedule that week for my funeral—that way, you'll only have to see me one more time. I'll be dead then, but I wouldn't want you to waste your vacation days on the person who had to drive an economy car so he could afford to pay for your guitar lessons."

    Your kid should now feel absolutely terrible, and will probably try to make amends by saying something like, "I wish I could visit longer. How about I e-mail you some pictures?" To which you'll reply, "I'd love some pictures—but my laptop is broken, and on my fixed income, I can't afford another one." Then pause, expel a few wheezy breaths, and go for the close: "Do you know where I might get a new laptop, son?" If he tries to say something like, "But I've just gotten you a top-of-the-line humidifier," immediately start gagging on phlegm. As you gasp for air, tell him that the doctor thinks he may have found a polyp in your prostate (you'd send him a picture of it, but. . .). By then, all you should hear is, "Do you want a PC or a Mac?"

WHO KNEW I COULD RAISE SUCH AN UNGRATEFUL CHILD?

Guilt is the foundation of a healthy parent-child relationship. Make sure that, this year, your Mother's Day or Father's Day is more than a vase of dying flowers and the all-you-can-eat buffet. Make sure that, this year, your kids know what you've gone through to keep them out of prison. While you appreciate a card that plays "Close to You" when you open it, if they want to say thank-you, they can do it with a plane ticket to your son's spare bedroom—one way.

SURVIVAL TIPS

1. Feel free to be demanding on your special day. There is no reason you've got to spend Mother's Day or Father's Day at brunch if you'd prefer that your kids take you to an RV liquidation sale.

2. Developing a good hacking cough is a very important part of the guilt trip. It's recommended that you go to parks and other public places to practice coughing. If you can get people to stop and ask if you're okay, you'll be ready for your kid's phone call.

3. Feel free to use the guilt trips included in this chapter . . . or don't. They were written for you to give someone a guilt trip. But if you don't want to, that's fine. It just means they were created for nothing.

PART

VIII

WEDDINGS
(NOT JUST FOR GREEN CARDS ANYMORE)

chapter 20

IT'S MY WEDDING, SO WHY IN THE HELL ARE YOU CRYING?

Marriage is ever made by destiny.

· GEORGE CHAPMAN ·

. . . Sometimes that destiny includes your sister being pissed because you sat her at the table with your co-workers.

One of the main reasons people get married is to start a family better than the ones they came from. They may *think* they're marrying each other because they're good looking, funny, or pregnant. The truth is, this new union is an opportunity to start a family that doesn't condone chewing tobacco at the dinner table. It's a fresh start with which to teach kids that it's not okay to use the F-word—even if it is the weekend. Your wedding is the first day of a brand-new life. It's special. That's why your family is driven to destroy it.

Just because our families are invited to the wedding, or help to plan or pay for it, they think it's somehow about them. It's like showing up at your company picnic and being angry because you haven't been made CEO for bringing the deviled eggs. To make sure our families don't interfere with our special day, we must take action. Specifically, there's a three-step solution that virtually guarantees a great wedding. Let's take a look at the first and most important step: the sarcastic e-mail.

THE PREEMPTORY SARCASTIC E-MAIL

More than any creative seating of the family drunks, placating pissed-off parents, or soothing the bruised egos of bridesmaids, the single most effective tool we have is to simply send out a sarcastic and threatening e-mail message. Included is a sample e-mail you can use as the basis for addressing your family.

To: wouldbeweddingruiners@hergiftregistrysucks.com
From: Alisa.Stack@bossycow.com
Re: Andrew Short marrying Alisa Stack

Hi everyone:
We're almost to the big day. I know some of you are so happy for me, you can hardly bring yourselves to return my phone calls. To make sure everyone at the wedding is as happy to be there as I am, I've got a few special requests. For my oldest sister and the maid of honor, Bernice: You are in charge of feeling weird that your younger sister is getting married before you. Please express this feeling in the form of mean comments right before I walk down the aisle. As you hand me the bouquet, whisper in my ear that I am a fat, ugly pig. I won't think you're projecting your own self-image onto me. Since you're my sister, I'll just consider it tough love. Also, feel free to call my fiancé a bastard to his face. I'll let him know that absorbing undeserved insults is a Stack family tradition.
Speaking of my fiancé, I know there are several people on his side of the family who were hoping he'd marry Shari Coffinstini—whose parents are

both successful lawyers. I am sorry your dream didn't come true. If only Shari weren't a lesbian, there may have been a chance. But don't lose hope. There is still a chance of being related to the Coffinstinis—I've noticed that your youngest daughter is quite the golfer.

I do wish I came from a family as rich as yours, but since I am much better looking than your son, I think it balances out. A piece of ass like me with money would be out of his league.

My special request is that you get so drunk, you forget that I'm insisting on keeping my last name.

To my mom: You are in charge of hating the flowers. When you talk about how terrible they look, please do so loudly, and in view of the videographer. I'm sorry we couldn't let you plan more of the wedding. Remember, the deal was that you could handle the floral arrangements if you agreed to take your lithium in front of a witness. You obviously love the voices in your head more than your daughter.

To my dad: The saying, "Just be yourself," does not apply to you. Please be anyone but yourself. Especially don't be the part of yourself who likes to argue about religion. You know it's going to be a Catholic wedding. If you pass out condoms as you've threatened to do, I'll let Mom know about the time I caught you and our neighbor Frank trying on her clothes.

To friends of the groom: Please refrain from being too aggressive towards the single women (except for Bernice—we'll name our first kid after anyone brave enough to tap that).

Other than that, thank you so much for being part of our special day. It's going to be a lot of fun! Remember, the theme of the wedding is "ocean"—so let me apologize in advance to those of you who are still mourning Uncle Carl. We had no idea about the boating accident.

Sincerely,
Alisa Stack

I'LL NEED TO SEE SOME ID

The above letter should hopefully shame your family into keeping cool (or piss them off to the point of not attending—either way, you win). What you must then plan for are the relatives who become irate but still show up. These are probably the same folks who were going to cause trouble anyway, so the fact that you've given them a bit of ammunition won't matter once you employ the second phase of the plan: hire some bouncers. If your sister stands up from dinner and yells, "Yuck! I hate fish," your rent-a-thug can drag her out of the reception by her braided pigtails, and toss her into a nearby koi pond. Nothing keeps a wedding peaceful like roving ex-cons wearing blood-stained pants.

A WEDDING IS NO PLACE TO GET MARRIED

The last step is to get married beforehand. Do you really want to spend one of the most important days of your life being upstaged by an obnoxious drunk or a cute flower girl (who hopefully aren't the same person)? Remember, a perfect marriage is the start of a brand-new life. So fly to Vegas and do it right. If the letter and the bouncers fail to keep your new brother-in-law from calling your mom a sexy bitch, it really won't matter. By the power vested in Elvis, you're already husband and wife.

HAPPILY EVER AFTER

It's not unreasonable to expect a perfect wedding if we're willing to be manipulative and heavy-handed. Believe it or not, your parents (and other relatives) want you to prevent them from ruining your wedding. Chances are, your grandparents ruined their wedding. You can now put an end to the cycle of matrimonial abuse. Not only will you have a beautiful wedding, you'll be a pioneer. It's like being the first person in your family to go to college—except your dad won't hate you for trying to be better than him.

SURVIVAL TIPS

1. Your family doesn't really want to ruin your wedding. They just don't know any better. You should see your relatives as having the same plight as homeless drug addicts—they didn't mean to end up this way, they just fell in with the wrong crowd.

2. No matter how charming or handsome they are, never let the bouncers dance with your guests. It's hard to ask a guy to throw your cousin out if he's made plans with her to hook up later.

chapter 21

I CAN'T BELIEVE I'M PAYING FOR HER TO MARRY HIM

Marriage is the mother of the world.

· DR. JEREMY TAYLOR ·

. . . I think he left off a word at the end of mother.

If your daughter (or son) is marrying into a family that thinks Good Friday is the day truck drivers post SHOW ME YOUR TITS signs in their windows, you've only got yourself to blame. If you'd done a better job instilling classist values, your kid might've considered the person she's about to marry to be nothing more than a fun little fling. Instead, you filled your kid's head full of crap like, "Marry who you love" or "Find someone who makes you happy." You screwed up. And now your little darling is marrying a guy who responds to the question, "What do you want to do as a career?" with, "Well, right now, I help people park their cars at rock concerts."

Watching your daughter marry into a family who can spend hours swapping stories about which frozen french fries cook the fastest isn't going to be easy. But never fear, with a little preparation you'll be able to smile at your future "family"—and almost mean it.

THE PARENTS' WEDDING PLANNER

Chances are, you've already met the "other" family. You may have known each other for a few months. They've grown comfortable enough with you to put you on their dirty-joke e-mail distribution list. Or you could've just caught your first glimpse of these people at the rehearsal dinner—and were quite impressed when their fifty-five-year-old Great-Grandma Tungus ate a twenty-ounce steak in under a minute—winning the bet. Either way, you may think you know enough about these people to control yourself during your daughter's special day. Think again. The wedding will confront you with the reality that these people can now say, "The Mullvaneys? Heck, yeah, we're related to 'em! My boy knocked one of 'em up."

To make sure the wedding decorum doesn't end up including yellow police tape, you need some exercises to harden yourself against what you'll be facing at the wedding:

- *Bums, hobos, and street performers:* It's a sad reality that our country has so many who are homeless. However, they can help you prepare for your kid's big day. Prior to the wedding, walk up to a homeless guy and ask him how work is going, what his hobbies are, and if he'd like to shoot a round of golf sometime. He'll probably just ask you for a dollar to buy some booze— which is probably the same reaction you'd get from your new relatives.

- *Do you feel lucky, punk?* Another great thing to do is walk up to some teenage punk and tell him he can call you "Dad." He may ask, "How about I call you Shithead?" After enduring this abuse, you'll be downright thankful if all your new son-in-law does is compliment you for raising a real wildcat of a daughter.

Likewise, you can grow accustomed to a less-than-ideal future daughter-in-law by walking into a nail salon, finding some vapid, bubble-blowing babe, and saying, "Welcome to the family." She'll probably reply, "Wow! I've always wanted to meet my real dad." Ignore any impulse to complete her fantasy and stay focused on getting through to the next day.

THE WEDDING DAY

No matter how thoroughly you prepare, you may still get caught off guard by the behavior of your new family. When you can't stand to watch another break-dancing contest or listen to your new relatives shout requests that the DJ play something by Tool so as to lighten the mood, there's one final yet extreme trick: pretend your new relatives are all mentally challenged (some of you won't have to pretend). In an instant, you'll go from being annoyed to being impressed at their ability to function in society. You won't try to ignore them; you'll want to film a documentary about them. Most important, it will allow you to take your mind off the fact that you may soon have a grandkid who stares up at you through the same pair of low-set hereditary horse-eyes that are now being used by the groom's father to check out your wife.

SHOULD I CALL YOU "DAD" OR "DUDE"?

When the big day arrives, be proud of yourself for not flipping out. It takes a big man to stand by while his hard-earned money's being used to sponsor a burping contest. If you feel yourself becoming annoyed, just remember to breathe and relax. The last thing you want to do is break down and start cursing at everyone. You're liable to hear one of your new in-laws say, "See? He's just like us."

SURVIVAL TIPS

1. Remember that your new relatives are just like you. They put their pants on one leg at a time—except when they answer the door.

2. Look on the bright side: they say intelligence skips a generation, so chances are, if your daughter's highly intelligent, you didn't have much to lose.

3. Respect the talents of your new in-laws. The ability to make your own Band-Aids may not seem like much, but it's very useful when there's a good chance your grandchild's first words will be "knife," "What's that green string under my skin?" and "Uh-oh. Where's the sewing kit?"

chapter 22

I HOPE SHE TRIPS ON HER DRESS
(FOR OVERWORKED SIBLINGS OF THE BRIDE)

Marriage—a book of which the first chapter
is written in poetry and the remaining chapters
written in prose.

· BEVERLEY NICHOLS ·

. . . And if there were a chapter written
by the bride's sister, it'd just be a collection
of old slave spirituals.

We don't start out wishing that in addition to getting something old, something new, something borrowed, and something blue, our soon-to-be married sisters would also get food poisoning. The desire to watch them hurl all over the flower girl is developed over weeks and months of indentured sibling servitude. At first, we're happy for our sisters (not to be sexist, but women care way more about their wedding day than men. If weddings were about men, "I do" would be replaced with, "Sure, what the hell?"). In the beginning, she only makes acceptable requests: go shopping for rubber penises (because what's a bachelorette party without repeated acts of simulated fellatio?), or help her score some diet pills. But before you know it, she's asking you to culture bacteria for homemade yogurt (she can't eat store-bought yogurt—not before *her* wedding); or if you'd be a honey and go milk a cow, because she's got a yearning for fresh cream.

Let's take a look at some methods for resisting the tyranny of a betrothed sibling:

BE A DEAR AND GET ME AN IVORY TUSK
(AND OTHER UNREASONABLE DEMANDS)

If you're lucky, your sister will have chosen her roommate from college to be her maid of honor (or "mad ho" for short). This means you'll be relegated to bridesmaid status. If your sister asks you to be a sweetie and buy her some ground-up rhinoceros horn to use as an aphrodisiac on her wedding night, you can say, "Why don't you ask your mad ho? I'm in charge of the strippers, not violating the Endangered Species Act just so your husband won't have to spend the evening apologizing."

If you are both her sister *and* mad ho, you can expect a workload that would make a migrant laborer wince. In fact, if Jimmy Hoffa had been a woman whose sister was about to be married, you can bet your ass there'd be a Maid of Honor's Union (the AFL-CI-HO).

So why not take a page from unionized labor? If your sister comes at you with yet another unreasonable request to be a darling and install a garage-door opener in her new townhouse, just let her know that if she makes one more outlandish demand, you're going to organize a walkout with all the other bridesmaids. You can even threaten to picket her house. Chances are, it'll never come to your taking action, but just suggesting that her diva attitude is about to cause a revolt will be enough to get her to back off.

Perhaps the most powerful defense is the threat of giving an embarrassing or bad toast. Find a subtle way to let your sister know that how she treats you will have a direct effect on the number of times in your toast you will say, "I can't believe how much weight she's lost." If she's demanding you wear a dress that'll reveal your back tattoo to the entire family, let her know that, in your toast, you'll be sure to mention to every aunt and grandma present, "If you think *my* tattoo is risqué, you should see where the bride has a tattoo of the Microsoft Paperclip!" ("I notice you are engaging in foreplay, can I help you with that?")

"MY NAME IS RACHEL!" NO. YOUR NAME IS KUNTA KINTE

You need not fear being exploited by a soon-to-be married sister. If you two get into a tiff, just ask her how she'll feel about spending her bachelorette party with scab labor. And if that fails to move her toward being a bit more reasonable in her requests, make sure she knows that if she doesn't relent, you'll praise her new husband during the toast as "a man who isn't afraid of a few little herpes."

SURVIVAL TIPS

1. Never let your soon-to-be-married sister try to make you feel jealous of her impending marriage. It's just a ploy to manipulate you into doing even more, as well as a way for her to feel like the guy she's marrying is special enough to warrant jealousy (no matter how many times you tell her you aren't into dudes with chronic fatigue syndrome).

2. If your sister looks great in her wedding dress, be sure to tell people that she can thank the TrimSpa and Red Bull diet for her hot body—and for her next five years of heart palpitations.

3. No matter what, remember that being your sister's bridesmaid is an honor—unless it's her second marriage, in which case it's just a round-about way of asking you to help her move.

chapter 23

WHAT DO YOU MEAN JEWS DON'T CELEBRATE CHRISTMAS?
(INTERFAITH MARRIAGES)

If I had to choose a religion, the sun as the universal giver of life would be my god.

· NAPOLEON BONAPARTE ·

. . . And if I had to choose a religion to marry into, I'd become an agnostic.

Religion plays a large part in a family's identity (like the Manson family, for example). Nowhere is this clearer than at weddings. Even families who aren't "religious" often want their relatives to have a traditional wedding, if for no other reason than to keep the grandparents from flinging themselves off a bridge. When news first spreads through a family that little Sally O'Malley is marrying Hussein Abu Ghraib, both sides ask, "Is it going to be a Catholic wedding?" or "Is it going to be a Muslim wedding?" Some family members are happy that the youngsters have found love, while

others are still sore about the Crusades and consider this union akin
to the Roadrunner marrying Wile E. Coyote (of course, Wile E.
Coyote was always trying to build bombs with which to blow up the
Roadrunner—but he was just in love and confused).

However, even the most enlightened family members may gag a
bit when they witness a ceremony combining aspects of two faiths. On
the surface, they may be prepared to accept an avant-garde wedding.
That is, until they actually witness a ceremony during which, right
after the bride and groom take communion, they face Mecca and pray.

HOW COULD SHE DO THIS TO HER GRANDMOTHER?

Many people often wonder how an interfaith union starts in the first
place. Here are a few reasons you could soon have an "other" side of
the family:

■ *Her family didn't do a good enough job teaching that* her *religion is
   the only true path to Heaven:* If they'd properly instilled in her that
   so much as shaking hands with someone of another faith is sure
   condemnation to Hell, the rest of her family wouldn't be preparing to spend three hours at the Morgenstein-Andrews wedding
   saying, "You know, I have a friend who's Jewish." (And chances
   are, they'll be referring to Jesus.)
■ *Her family pushed too hard to turn her into a good Catholic, Jew,
   or Muslim and it backfired:* Sometimes, even when a family does
   the right thing by cloistering their child in a world of parochial
   school, all that happens is that they end up rebelling. They marry
   someone of another faith just to pay their parents back for twelve
   years of plaid-skirt hell at the Our Lady of Repression Academy
   (of course, whoever she marries will probably ask that she keep
   her schoolgirl uniform to wear on special occasions).

■ *An unmet need to have spiritual meaning in their lives:* Occasionally, nonreligious parents will give birth to a kid who longs for some sort of spiritual meaning. If they're too busy taking sensual-massage classes to at least send her to Bible camp, she'll end up finding her spiritual path through someone else—and that someone else may have her praying five times a day that Allah destroy all Disney movies.

And a few lesser but still completely reasonable ways that interfaith unions happen:

■ *On the first date, her fiancé threw a stick on the ground and it turned into a snake:* That's enough to make anyone convert.
■ *While driving, she saw one of those* COEXIST *bumper stickers and fell for it:* People often undervalue the power of bumper stickers. If a person is in the right emotional state, seeing a message in front of him at fifty-five mph can cause an epiphany (and hopefully not a seven-car pileup—though it would be hard not to also interpret that as a sign).

IS IT TRUE YOU PEOPLE PRAY TO A SACK OF POTATOES NAMED SPUDTHARTA?

A big part of surviving interfaith weddings (and having new family from a different religion, for that matter) is making sure we understand a bit about our newly imposed relatives. Let's review a few of the basics:

Christianity

■ First, some little-known historical background: The celebration of Christmas actually began as a gay pride parade. However, the major gay elements of Christmas, like decorating things, singing in the streets and the symbolism of the chimney, were combined with the celebration of the birth of Jesus to make it a more mean-ingful holiday. Without Jesus, Christmas would be totally gay.

■ Christians don't just believe Jesus died for their sins; they also believe he died for the right to party (the Beastie Boys have con-tinued to fight for this right as well). If your new Presbyterian or Catholic relatives are really hitting the "Jesus Juice," they're just enjoying a benefit of their faith. It's no different than Jewish mothers' enjoying the right to become hysterical over absolutely nothing.

Judaism

■ When you meet a new Jewish relative, it is customary to bow, not so much as a sign of respect as to accommodate their stereotypi-cally short stature. Should you meet a tall Jew, you should still bow. He'll then say, "Oy, does your back hurt?" and recommend a good chiropractor—who will no doubt be a cousin, uncle, or brother.

Hinduism

■ It is not just a stereotype; every single Hindu person is in some way connected to the convenience-store industry: It's actually how they practice their religion. The Hindu God is an eight-armed elephant capable of stocking every shelf at once. When they restock the Funyuns, they're restocking their souls.

■ If the wedding involves a Hindu ceremony, do not be surprised if the groom comes out riding an elephant or horse: If it's a horse, resist asking which style he prefers riding in, Western or English. You may start a hunger strike.

Muslim

- If your new Muslim relatives must fly to get to the wedding, you may want to allow an extra day or two so they have a chance to get through security (or get released from Guantanamo).
- Those of us in the West don't know much about their prophet Muhammad. The most important thing to remember is that his name used to be Cassius Clay, and he was the undefeated Heavyweight Champion of the World. All that talk of anticonsumerism from much of the Muslim world is really just anger at the success of the grill endorsed by his rival, George Foreman.
- Despite the bad press, most Muslims are peaceful people. It's only a fraction of their population who chant, "Death to America." The rest shout, "Death to hybrid vehicles."

Whatever Chinese People Are

- Chinese people number in the trillions, so there's a good chance someone from your family will end up marrying a #27 (Biology major with sense-of-humor sauce). You won't know if your new Chinese family is Buddhist, Taoist, Islamic, Christian, or Falun Gong. So the best thing to do is ask. If he says, "I'm Shinto, you moron," it means he's actually Japanese and you owe him an apology.

What the Hell Did He Just Step On?

Even with all of our newfound religious understanding, there can still be aspects of interfaith wedding ceremonies that can shock us. Here are just a few peculiarities you may want to prep yourself for:

- *Jewish weddings:* The groom is going to break a glass during the ceremony (if it's a Hindu-Jewish wedding, the elephant is permitted to break the glass). This tradition comes from years of accusing Jews of being cheap. It says to the attendees, "I'm cheap, huh? Well, watch me destroy this perfectly good piece of stemware."

- *Greek weddings:* No matter what, never yell, "When are you ass-holes going to stop dancing!?" The famous Greek circle dance symbolizes the shape of a folded gyro and is a sacred ritual.
- *Catholic weddings:* Catholic weddings are long. Prepare to go without food for such a length of time that all you'd need were a couple of rugs and a sunset to turn it into a day of Ramadan. If you try to smuggle food in, never bring sausages. The cas-ings may be mistaken for condoms—and if those were allowed, chances are, you wouldn't be at this wedding in the first place.
- *Muslim weddings:* Don't be surprised if there's a space just for women to practice Hijab (the veiling or seclusion of women). Just because a man is marrying a woman doesn't mean everyone else has to catch cooties.

IT'S IMPORTANT TO EXORCISE RELIGIOUSLY

With a little understanding, you'll feel right at home no matter what barbaric rite you're forced to witness. Remember, no matter if you're Hindu, Buddhist, Presbyterian, Lutheran, Jewish, Muslim, Wiccan, or a Branch Davidian, there is one thing we all have in common: we're not Zoroastrian. Those people are freaks.

SURVIVAL TIPS

1. Knowing a bit about your new family's religion will help not only in getting through the wedding ceremony, but with future interactions as well. Should you see new Jewish relatives next Easter, you'll know better than to ask, "Isn't this about the time of year you guys killed Christ? And why don't you celebrate that, again?"

2. If some of the older relatives absolutely cannot process the fact that their proud Muslim daughter just said "I do" in front of Father O'Leary, just convince them that the ceremony is just a mirage.

3. Accept the fact that, upon hearing that one of their relatives is marrying into another religion, some family members will not have been so upset since they learned *The Da Vinci Code* was a best seller. We will always have a relative who keeps sending her grandkid sweaters emblazoned with a cross, no matter how many times we tell her he's studying to be a rabbi.

chapter 24

BRANDON, DO YOU TAKE SHANIQUAH TO BE YOUR WIZIFE?
(INTERRACIAL WEDDINGS)

Yellow and blue make green.

· ZIPLOC ·

. . . Yeah, but yellow's parents disowned him,
and we all know from Kermit the Frog that
"It ain't easy being green."

Ideally, this chapter shouldn't have to be written. We should never have to think twice if our son marries a hot Latina who reminds him of his childhood nanny. Nor should we ever have to worry about how we're going to explain to Honorable Grandma that her precious Kim-Lee Chung has found her feng shui with Federico, her Puerto Rican driving-school instructor. However, this book would be delinquent in its family-gathering preparation if we didn't discuss such things as how to handle accidentally using the words "you" and "people" back to back while meeting Shaniquah's cousins for the first time.

(Note: if you do accidentally refer to your new black relatives as "you people" and they come back with, "What do you mean, 'you people'?" just reply with, "You people who are soon to be family," then change the subject to sports.)

SOME KNOWLEDGE TO DROP BEFORE YOU TIE THE KNOT

First of all, if you're about to welcome some new and exciting race into your family, congratulations! You may soon have your very own Tiger Woods. An interracial family is great but, unlike plain old uniracial couples, biracial couples have a few more premarriage details to attend to:

- *Ultimate fighting:* If you're planning on starting an interracial family, one of the first things you should do is consider how you'll prepare a kid for all the fights he'll get into. Mixed-race kids are better than plain old vanilla, chocolate, or strawberry kids (despite the going rate for a white baby on the Mexican black market). Other kids know this, so they will tease and pick on them mercilessly. Your child must be prepared to defend himself.

  These days, mixed martial arts is a very popular form of combat. If you invest in your child's ability to beat up would-be name callers, he can answer "How was school?" with: "It was great! I got an A on my math test, and I put Tim Russell in a headlock for calling me a latte-face."

- *All in the family:* It is an unfortunate and sad reality that some family members will not approve of an interracial union. But that doesn't mean we can't change their minds. To convert backwards family members, try creating a "hero moment." A hero moment is when you put the family member's life in jeopardy and then have your partner save them. For example, you love Juan and don't care that your mother says he's using you for a green card. When your mom leaves her house one day to buy country music CDs, saw through the stair banisters to within a splinter of breaking off. When she returns, have Juan waiting under the stairs. She'll try walking up, and when she reaches for the banister, she'll fall within an inch of cracking her hip, only to be caught in the firm hands of Juan, her soon-to-be son-in-law. It's hard to hate someone if he's saved your life.

(If she's only got a single-story house with no stairs, you can cut the brake lines in your mom's car, so long as you're sure Juan is capable of driving up beside her on a motorcycle and yelling "Jump!")

■ *Meeting her father:* We should also make sure the interracial couple is getting married for the right reasons. If Shaniquah has brought home a "Brandon," there are two explanations: Shaniquah's father has told her not to date white guys, and she's rebelling. Or Shaniquah's family raised her correctly to believe that people are people, and she fell in love with Brandon because they both enjoy listening to Lenny Kravitz and watching Halle Berry movies. If it's the latter, Brandon and Shaniquah will live happily ever after. And so long as Brandon is never caught mouthing the lyrics to any rap songs, her family will accept him.

If he's nothing more than a human middle finger to her parents, then homeboy can get ready for a rough relationship!

SAY WHAT?

For most interracial unions, no topic will be off-limits. But because of the strained work relations between blacks and whites about two hundred years ago, there are a few guidelines that Afro-Caucasoid conversations should adhere to:

Never talk about affirmative action with new black relatives. It's not that both sides can't have an intelligent conversation; it's just that any discussion of past inequalities can pretty much guarantee that, during Christmas and family gatherings to come, you will not get any help clearing the table or doing the dishes, based on principle.

In the beginning of a conversation, I recommend talking about sports for no more than fifteen minutes. Any more than that and you may insult your new black relative by implying that he has no other interests. Also, sports are going to be our conversation saver later in the reception, should we stumble into dangerous topics. If your oldest son brings up Jesse Jackson, you can quickly say, "Don't you mean Reggie Jackson [the Hall of Fame baseball player]?"

Here is a list of additional topics *never* to discuss: (1) What color was Jesus? (2) Politics, (3) Al Sharpton, (4) Michael Richards, and (5) What the hell is Kwanzaa?

Topics that are safe for discussion include: (1) Oprah, (2) Raising kids, (3) Shopping, (4) O. J. Simpson (*everyone* thinks he's guilty), and (5) Sports.

PLANNING AN INTERRACIAL WEDDING

An interracial wedding is just like any other wedding, except for a few small details:

■ *Music:* Rap or metal? Mariachi or the blues? The music you choose can play a large part in making your guests feel comfortable. If you play too much Guns N' Roses, it may be difficult to convince the other side of the family to go out on the floor and slam-dance with their new relatives. Likewise, dropping some hip-hop tracks on the classic-rock set will at most inspire a few ill-attempted cabbage patches and running men. No one wants to see that.

If you can't decide on music that matches the tastes of both sides of the family, then choose music that isn't from either of your backgrounds. It's better to have no one dancing to Slavic yodeling than watching half the party line-dance to Charley Pride.

■ *Seating:* Unless you want your wedding reception to look like a bus from 1950s Alabama, it's best to make sure equal numbers of both families are seated at each table.

■ *Themes and religion:* Even if both sides are of the same faith, there will no doubt be different customs and traditions each will insist on having in the ceremony. Rather than try to make both sides happy, you should choose a theme that can unite the party. So, for a black-white union, why not have a Civil War–themed wedding? Have the pastor dress as Abraham Lincoln. After the bride and groom say their vows, he can set one side of the family free, and the other side of the family can pretend to be Yankees welcoming them to settle in Harlem.

For any half-Latino wedding, use the piñata to build a bridge. If it's a Mexican-Arab wedding, make the piñata in the shape of the Middle East and, when you break it open, have sand and oil pour out (but don't have it explode—that'd be taking it a bit too far).

Can't we All Just Get Hitched?

Interracial marriage wasn't even legal in some states until 1967, and since then, the number of interracial couples has doubled every decade. If you or a member of your family is about to add to the trend, remember that not only are you finding love, you're helping to copulate an end to racism. Now, go piss off your parents!

SURVIVAL TIPS

1. The interracial couple must name their children after the family members who disapprove of their union—because irony can heal all wounds.

2. If you accidentally say what could be perceived as a racist comment (i.e., wet white people smell like puppies), just apologize and say that you heard it in a rap song.

3. If you and your spouse should ever break down and yell racial epithets at each other during a fight, and the neighbors overhear it, just tell them you were watching a Spike Lee movie.

IX

GET ME SOME WARM BLANKETS AND A SHOTGUN

(SURVIVING HAVING A BABY)

chapter 25

GET OUT OF THE DELIVERY ROOM, BITCH!
(AND OTHER TENDER MOTHER-DAUGHTER MOMENTS)

The tie which links mother and child
is of such pure and immaculate strength
as to be never violated.

· WASHINGTON IRVING ·

. . . Until grandmother shows grandchild
the benefits of eliminating the middleman.

If you were at an airport waiting for someone special to arrive,
would you let anyone tell you that you couldn't stand at the end of
the gate? Wouldn't you want to be there when that person passed
through the jetway and into your life? If someone told you to leave,
you'd be like, "Piss off! I'm waiting for my friend."

That's exactly how grandparents feel about the delivery room.
They don't want to pick up the baby at the curbside; they want to

be standing in front of the womb in a limo suit with a sign that says "Granddaughter" or "Grandson."

Unfortunately, we can't always oblige them. If they'd actually behave like they say they're going to, it'd be different. But parents always think they need to be parenting, even when *we're* the ones about to become parents. If you think your mom's controlling when you set the table at Thanksgiving, just wait until she yells at the doctor for not setting up his tool tray with the scalpel blade facing in, to the right of the forceps.

And it's a lot more complicated than simply asking your mother to leave. You may think this is a beautiful day for you, but having a child is a very special moment in your *parents'* lives. To them, you aren't an expectant mother; you're just a grandchild-delivery device. Your womb is nothing more than a window in the space-time continuum, through which the next member of *their* family travels on its way to Nana and Grampy's house. They aren't at the hospital to help you. They've come to collect their grandchild.

The same goes for your in-laws. As far as they're concerned, the only reason their son married you was to try to improve the gene pool. You exist solely to replace their hereditary hook-noses with your perfect little button shnoz. You aren't a person, you're a parts dispenser.

When you consider all of this, it's easy to see how your family can ruin the birthing process. What makes it even worse is that when you're about to deliver, you're often too vulnerable to defend yourself. Even if you muster up the energy to ask your mom for some privacy, she'll just come back and say, "When I was pregnant, I let *you* in the delivery room."

Don't let them turn you into a baby kiosk, or your delivery into a spectator sport! Here are some fun ways to fight back:

PROTRACTED LABOR TALKS

Husbands are our primary defense against intrusive family members. Before we look at how to use them to safeguard our deliveries, let's first understand a bit about who we're working with:

■ *Men don't understand why you can't just decide when to start your contractions.* To him, you're stalling. Your delayed contractions are no different than the times he stands outside the bathroom yelling, "Come on! You said you'd be ready to go to dinner an hour ago." He thinks that you're simply being fashionably late; that you can start having the baby anytime you want, but rather than do it when you're refreshed, you'd prefer to wait until you haven't slept in thirty hours. Therefore, you must immediately explain that you can't control when your contractions start. To make sure he doesn't try heading back to the office, tell him it's like a rain delay in baseball, and to go sit in the dugout till he hears his name called.

■ *Most men have developed a biological resistance to women's feelings.* This is an important adaptation, allowing men to experience happiness—but when it comes to being a good birthing partner, it will leave him unable to empathize. To make sure he's there for you, it's recommended that you trick him into wearing estrogen patches. If he smokes, tell him they're a new kind of nicotine patch that replaces the craving for tobacco with the craving to listen to you and understand your feelings. And don't worry about the side effects—your dude's always playing with your breasts. Soon he'll have a set of his own.

Now let's look at two examples of how a husband is used to defend your delivery-room sovereignty.

I'll Need To See Your Credentials

When your older sister was in labor, your dad took pictures as she projectile-vomited off the side of the bed. Now he carries around a picture in his phone entitled "Pukerella," which he shows to all his friends (usually after a few beers, when one of them asks, "What's the grossest thing you've ever seen in your life?"). You've vowed not to suffer the same fate.

What do you do about a parent or relative who's obviously never gotten over his youthful desire to shave off one of his drunken friends' eyebrows? How do you block a parent who considers your pregnancy to be a fraternity prank?

The answer is to let the entire family know that your husband's the only one with a press pass to the delivery room. If your dad (or any belligerent relative) so much as pulls out a cell phone, ask that nurse who looks like she might have recently been stripped of her Olympic medals to escort him out. Then you can rest assured that the only one with the ability to record the events of the birth is your husband (and if he takes a picture of you vomiting, at least you'll know where you get your taste in men).

Mom, Have You Seen The Hospital's Gift Shop?

Initially, you may have agreed to allow your parents or in-laws into the delivery room. You didn't want to deny them their joy. Plus, you were having an emotional spell at the time and not thinking clearly. Because of your desire to do the right thing (or your hormone-corrupted decision making), many of your relatives will be walking into the hospital carrying folding chairs and wearing giant foam fingers, eagerly expecting a great birthing event. Your mother has even been brushing up on her medical terminology, just in case the doctor needs her assistance.

The only problem is that our parents and in-laws just aren't mature enough to be in the delivery room. We *would* let them stay. But we can't take the risk of hearing a mother-in-law shriek, "Is that how you prepare the mother of my grandchild for giving birth! Don't any of you nurses know how to operate an electric razor?"

But you don't want to point to your mom or mother-in-law and say, "Throw that one out! She looked at me funny." Then watch as she screams, "But you said I could be in the delivery room!" as she's dispatched into the hallway. In fact, you aren't going to tell anyone to leave at all. Your husband is. And he's going to do it in a way that makes him look like an idiot, rather than you like a bitch.

First, give your guy a codeword like "pancakes" or "matricide," to indicate that you need the old lady removed. Once he hears his code-word, he'll say something like, "You know what? We forgot to feed the cat. In two years, we don't want to ask Junior, 'What sound does a cat make?' only to have him imitate a buzzing swarm of flies. Would you run home and feed it, Mom?" If an excuse like this doesn't help eject the unruly relative, pre-approve your husband to go to Defcon 5: When all else fails, have him look your mom in the eye and say, "If you don't leave, we may soon be celebrating a combo birthday-funeral." Notice that in saying this, he's basically your Cyrano de Bergerac puppet. But when all's said and done, he'll be the asshole, and you'll be able to happily hold your baby in your arms while your mother's a mile from your house, realizing that you don't even have a cat.

DID YOU WANT DELIVERY CONFIRMATION?

It's hard to fault soon-to-be grandparents for their excitement. And just like kids, their well-intentioned exhilaration often becomes too much to handle. That's why you must keep your husband by your side in case a relative needs a time-out. He'll see to it that your delivery room will be your sanctuary, not your sanitarium.

SURVIVAL TIPS

1. Don't worry if your family still manages to turn your child's delivery into an episode of *Jerry Springer*. Being born during a shouting match won't scar your child any more than the other things he'll soon experience as a member of your family.

2. Another relaxation technique that can help block out annoying relatives is to have a favorite song in your head that helps you connect with the birthing process. Recommended songs include Soft Cell's "Tainted Love" for undergoing an episiotomy, and Roy and Dale's "Happy Trails to You" for undergoing a C-section.

3. Having a child is a beautiful experience. To anticipate who might annoy you in the delivery room, think about how they might admire other works of beauty. If your mother-in-law is the kind of person who'd say, "That's the *Mona Lisa*—a famous Italian chick with a facial tick," you should prepare for the possibility that she may try to start the wave as your delivery heads into the final stretch.

chapter 26

I'M HAVING A KID, NOT OPENING A BED-AND-BREAKFAST

(FOR FAMILY MEMBERS WHO JUST WON'T LEAVE)

Checkout is at noon.

· THE HOLIDAY INN ·

. . . And you will be charged for any
missing towels or babies.

You wanted to start a family so that you'd have a house filled with laughter. But it's supposed to come from your kid, not some freeloading brother-in-law watching reruns of *Mama's Family.* You wanted the pitter-patter of little feet, but it wasn't supposed to be caused by your mother-in-law's sneaking into the kitchen to stress-eat. What starts as a relative's visit to offer help following the birth of a child can turn into an unending vacation at Camp Newborn.

If you'd known your family would try to stay this long, then in addition to hanging fighter-jet wallpaper in the baby's room, you'd have decorated the guest bedroom with a TV remote-control mobile for your dad. You'd have hung a sign in the side yard that reads, "For closet smokers only," so that when your mother-in-law sneaks out after dinner, she'd know you had been thinking of her.

That's not to say you don't appreciate the support. It's a great help to have someone cook, clean, and put your dishes away in new and exciting places, where they're never to be found again. But there comes a time when you'd rather risk ripping your C-section stitches getting your own food than ask your uncle, for the millionth time, to please leave while you breastfeed the baby.

PLEASE, MAKE YOURSELF AT HOME
(FOR A LIMITED AMOUNT OF TIME)

Let's take a look at the main reasons why relatives try to stick around, and what we can do to get them unstuck:

Your parents and in-laws feel that it's their duty to make sure you don't starve, spindle, or mutilate their grandchild.

If they leave, you'll surely mistake the baby's crying for a reaction to the tear-jerking part in *Titanic* when Leonardo DiCaprio becomes a lifetime member of the Polar Bear Club. They think you're a clueless, incompetent parent. If they turn their backs for a moment, you'll surely dangle the baby off the balcony by its legs. Even if they do appear to be helpful, bringing you that bowl of raviolis is nothing more than a clever trick to get you to hand them the baby.

Solution: The way to handle the relative who thinks we're incompetent is to call them on their fear. Have your husband go to the toy store and buy a plastic baby doll—the kind that has the easily removable arms and legs. Remove the limbs and stash them in the baby blanket. If your mother-in-law says, "Look how you're holding the baby! Do you want him to be cross-eyed?" suddenly drop one of the doll parts on the floor. Then look at her and say, "Whoops. It's a good thing you're here, or the baby would just fall apart!" The good news is, these relatives will always want to babysit, if only to take your child in for a physical.

Some relatives won't leave because visiting you and your new child is distracting them from their own problems.

Back at home, your parents would just sit around discussing who screwed up whose life. Your baby gives them something positive to focus on, rather than the fact that your dad gambled away their life savings. In much the way you and your siblings kept your folks' marriage together, their new grandchild helps them avoid discussing why "that old friend from high school" keeps text-messaging your mom.

Solution: This is finally an opportunity to put that theater class you took in college to use. You and your husband are going to stage a mock argument that's so upsetting, your relatives would actually feel more comfortable if they left. Typically, these family members only have the emotional capacity to deal with their own problems. If your house appears to be haunted with the same discontent as theirs, they've got no reason to stick around.

To make this work, let your husband know ahead of time that you'll be picking a "fight" with him when you know they're in earshot. Come out of nowhere and yell, "What do you mean you lost ten thousand dollars playing online poker?!!" Remember to argue about something similar to your relatives' problems. This will re-create the exact thing they're trying to hide from. Then your husband should say, "Well, maybe I wouldn't have to look for excitement online if you'd occasionally take a break from volunteering at the church to be my wife! Do you think orphans are the only ones with needs?" Before you know it, your folks will be packing up the car. They can experience this misery in the comfort of their own home. (But don't be surprised if your father-in-law quietly pulls you aside and asks, "So what's this online gambling thing?")

Your relative's a freeloader.

It could be some brother, cousin, or uncle who just happened to quit his job as a security guard the same day you went into labor. That means he has an unlimited amount of time in which to support you. This "support" will come in the form of eating your food, watching your expanded-basic cable, and taking a much needed vacation from his roommate, who gets all weird every time he eats his food without asking permission.

Solution: This couch tumor is welcome to stay, provided that he chips in a bit. And by "a bit," we mean refinishing the kitchen cabinets he's helping to empty, reupholstering the couch his ass has customized, and otherwise working harder than if he were to resume his career of standing around in a mall. The longer he stays, the greater the demands should be. Don't stop until he either builds an ark, or decides life would be better spent yelling at teenagers for smoking.

THE DIAPER DIASPORA

Don't feel bad about sending parents and other relatives home. Yes, they've cooked and cleaned. But you're the one who made the baby. You're the one who didn't take an epidural so that your "holistic" mother-in-law would be appeased. You're the one whose episiotomy stitches itch worse than the time you borrowed your sister's pantyhose. Besides, your baby needs some alone time with you, so he can cry, vomit, and make you wish your mother was around to help.

SURVIVAL TIPS

1. Even though relatives can make our home feel like a hotel, slipping a newspaper under the bedroom door will not be a clear enough hint to leave (unless it's covered in a white, anthraxy powder).

2. Be sure to educate pushy relatives about the dangers of shaken grandparent syndrome.

3. If you start to notice that your parents' mail is being forwarded to your address, it may be time to start asking friendly "please leave" questions such as, "Who's been watering your plants?" "I bet you can't wait to sleep in your own bed, huh?" or "Which do you think will come first: the rapture, an apocalypse, or a taxi to take you to the airport?"

PART

FAMILY REUNIONS, FIREWORKS, AND FAT RELATIVES WEARING THONG BIKINIS

(SURVIVING SUMMERTIME GET-TOGETHERS)

chapter 27

PICTURE SHOWERS, PIG EATERS, AND THE INHERITANCE RELAY-RACE

Family is the most important thing in the world.

· PRINCESS DIANA ·

. . . I guess that's why her husband tried to have so many of them.

Your reunion may be anywhere from twenty to two hundred people—depending on your family's thoughts about birth control, if there are any restraining orders, or whether the state where the majority of your family's from has a three-strikes rule. Just as no house party is complete without people passing out on the bathroom floor, there are a few essential activities that must be part of any family reunion:

1. *Picture-showing marathon:* One of the reasons you love family reunions is that you can show your relatives so many pictures, they'll soon feel like they've been standing right next to you all year. Nowadays, with cell phones and MP3 players that are

capable of storing thousands of photos, you can spend an entire day giving some cousin or in-law his much-desired window into your life. So why not make a game of it? Just like the dance marathons of olden-days television, a picture-showing marathon pairs up a shutterbug (you) with a relative who'd rather suffer ocular penetration than see a "before" picture of your bathroom remodel. The one who can keep his spectator the longest wins.

The contestants begin by showing pictures to disinterested relatives. The rules require you to tell the spectator some random detail about every picture. For example, if you're subjecting the viewer to three hundred shots of your Alaskan vacation, be sure to say something like, "And this is us standing in front of a dismembered musk ox. Did you know that the neck of a musk ox is so thick, it can jam a chainsaw, and that their fur is machine-washable?"

You'll know that you're winning if the viewer asks follow-up questions like, "Was it asleep when you caught it? Have you ever eaten musk-ox meat? What's that like?" You've somehow managed to engage him. But if the picture only elicits a "Wow" or "That's cool," it's game over. Your spectator would rather have his kneecaps removed with a grapefruit spoon than see another photo. Any minute now, he'll give you an excuse and walk away before you can say, "And this is us standing in front of an illegally caught blue whale. Did you know Greenpeace ships aren't built to withstand torpedoes?"

2. *Tying on the family feedbag (eating contests):* Eating with family is the equivalent of feeling comfortable enough around certain people to walk around in your underwear. It's a time when you can dispense with the formalities of the fork and knife, and just shove your face sow style into the macaroni salad. In fact, many families look forward to reunions just to see which relative takes the blue

ribbon for Best New Jowls. Even if you don't formally organize an eating contest, one will spontaneously occur the minute your well-insulated relatives realize there's ten of them and only five pies. You don't even have to tell your relatives that they're part of a contest. If horses don't know why they're running around a track, there's no need to alert your clan that they're being evaluated on quantity consumed, who can eat with his face closest to the plate, and who can get the most food onto a single fork without dropping anything (or warping the utensil).

3. *Inheritance relay-race:* One of the major challenges of a family reunion is getting the youngest to interact with the oldest. Grandparents love family reunions because they've made most of the people there. It's like being a painter and holding an exhibition of your work (except that if anyone finds one forgotten in a basement, he won't call Sotheby's). And they want to have fun, like everyone else. Old folks are just like kids, except that if you put them on seesaws, their phlebitis acts up. To help your elderly relatives enjoy the reunion more, play a game that gets both young and old interacting. Have an inheritance relay-race.

   To play a game of Get Great-Granny Gum Disease a Ginger Ale, pair up two or three younger family members with an older relative who's never gotten around to spending her nest egg. The event starts when Great-Granny Gum Disease says, "I'm thirsty." The three contestants now rush off to bring her a glass of ginger ale. The first one back must say, "Here you go, Granny Gum Disease!" However, the other two aren't out of the game yet. They just have to wait until she takes a sip. If the glass has too much ice, not enough ice, too many bubbles or no straw, the first person is disqualified. However, if the ginger ale is absolutely perfect and succeeds in masking her cat-food breath, she'll say something like, "When I was your age, I wanted to see the world.

What would you do if you had enough money to travel?" Not only will that kid have a new reason to like his senior relatives but, to the older folks, this'll sure beat sitting alone on a bench playing peekaboo with a sleeping infant.

Is It All Just a Big Game To You?

Normally, picture showers, pig eaters, and awkward, lonely relatives would ruin a reunion. This year, you'll just see it all as one big game. Think about it: the only difference between the way your family gorges and how a professional eater devours fifty hot dogs in five minutes is that he's on TV, becoming a world champion. It just so happens that your family trains purely for the love of the sport.

Survival Tips

1. It's common to have T-shirts made with slogans that commemorate the reunion. Show your family how much you care by suggesting slogans such as, "Thompson Reunion 2008! Our hereditary alcoholism makes us great!" or "Thompson Reunion 2008! We might go to jail, but can always make bail!"

2. Never waste your family's time with the antiquated watermelon-eating contest. Fruit should only be eaten if it's encased in a piecrust.

3. Don't feel bad if you're not interested in attending this year's festivities. Many of us would prefer having a stomach worm to attending a family reunion (at least then, there might be something that *wants* to eat the three-bean salad).

chapter 28

SUMMERTIME REUNIONS: HOW NOT TO NOTICE BOTOX INJECTIONS, BREAST REDUCTIONS, DRAMATIC WEIGHT GAIN OR LOSS, OR ANYTHING ELSE YOU CAN'T HELP BUT NOTICE

There but for the grace of God go I.

· JOHN BRADFORD ·

. . . And if I were you, I'd seriously think about getting a bikini wax.

One of the major problems with summertime get-togethers is an unfortunate lack of clothing. Unlike the winter holidays, when a sweater can help man-boobs pass for pectoral muscles, the way families dress during summertime gatherings leaves little to the imagination. Beyond the burden of knowing how many men in your family have their nipples pierced, you must also endure foreheads full of Botox, facelifts from South American discount doctors, and other exotic alterations. You won't know if you're visiting family, or a burn unit.

How do we not stare at a sibling whose stomach stapling has left him with enough extra skin to reupholster a couch? How do we not get distracted when our recently separated, fifty-year-old aunt shows up sporting a set of gigantic new breasts that make her look like a cross between Pamela Anderson and a raisin? The following six tips will give you the understanding, empathy, and tools to keep your lunch down and your eyes up at this year's Fourth of July or family reunion.

Six tips for Ignoring The Unignorable

1. Understand what drove your relatives to make dramatic changes in their appearance. A middle-aged man with a Botox injection is basically telling the world, "I'm willing to kill my face if some of you will still consider having sex with me." Likewise, unneeded breast implants are really attempted love implants (of course, there are times when breast implants are needed—like after surgery or when you catch your boyfriend looking at a voluptuous woman).

2. Unlike a relative who would die of embarrassment if you mentioned her facelift, preferring to maintain the illusion that fairies magically erased the last forty years of cigarettes and sun exposure, some family members actually *want* you to notice a change. Maybe your stepdad celebrated his fiftieth birthday by getting those calf-muscle implants he'd always wanted. You can be damn sure he's going to want you to say, "Wow, your calves sure are muscular. I bet you climb stairs like a mountain goat!" In these situations, pay a quick compliment and be sensitive to *why* he needs one. Your relative may be saying, "Look at my huge calves," but all you'll hear is, *"Now* who's getting picked last for basketball?"

3. Always be ready to compliment family members on something other than what they've changed. Saying to your Auntie Fran, "That's a great T-shirt. You really are '49% Bitch, 51% Angel,'" is a lot better than rudely yelling out, "Wow, your new breasts are gigantic! When we go swimming, I'm going to use you to paddle out."

4. If you get caught staring at Cousin Phil's Botox-saturated forehead for signs of life, cut yourself some slack. It's natural. Your mind is just trying to determine if he's had a stroke or cosmetic surgery. If someone catches you staring, just apologize and explain that when people stare, their minds are trying to make sense of something they don't understand. Right now, you're trying to understand if Phil's forehead makes him looks younger, or sleepy. What does he think, young women are going to see him and think, "Wow, check out that hot older guy who's about to take a nap."

5. Remember that there's probably something about you that your family is trying not to notice as well. Pay attention if, while walking around barefoot, relatives start asking if your sneakers are comfortable to wear. It's probably just a nice way of saying, "Your feet smell like you found them at a garage sale! Please put your shoes on." Be sensitive to your family's comfort. You may even want to acknowledge your offensive feet and offer to put your shoes on if Aunt Trina also agrees to mind your arachnophobia before putting on her bikini.

6. Just like food, leaving relatives out in the sun too long will make them spoil. The smell of summer isn't just freshly cut grass or suntan lotion. It's also fermented nana and ripe uncle. How do we deal with being in the proximity of relatives who can't stay outside for longer than twenty minutes without smelling like stacks

of Renaissance-fair costumes? First, know that it isn't their fault. They aren't really trying to bring back the bubonic plague. Help them (and their tent mates) by encouraging them to go swimming. Then find a kid with a squirt gun, fill it with liquid soap, and ready, aim, sanitize! (Now that's some good clean fun.) And finally, for the truly unbearable, just offer to spray them down with scented bug spray. If they ask why you're using the entire can on their armpits and asses, just tell them that should they get bitten, those are the last places they'll want to be seen scratching.

Notice Anything Different?

You will find following these six tips sets you free from feeling like you're spending your Fourth of July or family reunion with victims of a radiation spill. Keep in mind that there may be times when you'll want to notice things, like your ten-year-old niece's showing up to the picnic with a pierced tongue. But remember that for the majority of your family, making them feel bad about the color they've dyed their hair, or how poorly toothless Grandma Sophie's new dentures fit, can come back to bite you in the ass.

SURVIVAL TIPS

1. If your ex-model aunt now has lips big enough to plunge a clogged Olive Garden toilet, be sure to simply compliment her lipstick color. Don't ask if she wears cruelty-free makeup. Chances are, her yearly lip-gloss consumption has wiped out an entire jungle of monkeys.

2. Accept that summertime gatherings are like a crime scene: we're going to see things most people shouldn't. It's not just a reunion; it's an episode of *CSI: My Family.*

3. Know that it's perfectly natural to stare at weird things. If you get caught with your confused eyes studying your sister's nose job, just say, "Sorry for staring. It's just that the last time I saw a nose that beautiful, it was nudging me awake so I'd let it out to pee."

chapter 29

CAMPING WITH DUMMIES

Only you can prevent forest fires.

· SMOKEY THE BEAR ·

. . . You can also start forest fires—
so know your options.

If you think your family's tough to get along with at home, try leaving them stranded in the wilderness covered with dirt and mosquito bites. Most families get testy if the pizza delivery driver is ten minutes late, or they have trouble finding parking at the movie theater. Do we really think these people can handle the stress of poorly pitched tents, antiquated, water-attracting sleeping bags, and siblings who think three months of guitar lessons qualify them to be the local minstrels whenever someone starts a campfire? Probably not. So, should you find yourself stranded in the woods with people who think "poison ivy" is a new perfume by Liz Taylor, the following tips should help:

WHERE TO PITCH YOUR TENT

Always try to pitch your tent next to the family who thinks camping is nothing more than a week of partying in the woods. This family should have a mixture of marijuana smoke and four-letter words billowing out of their campsite. The most important thing is to make sure these people are more obnoxious than your family, so that if anyone complains to the park ranger, it will be about them. A good sign that you've pitched your tent next to the right family is if you hear some mom yell, "Austin, come here and put your diaper back on, ya little son-of-a-bitch!"

WHAT TO PACK

Forget the usual canteens and gas grills; here is what you really need:

- *Hairspray and a lighter:* If you get bored, you and your youngest niece can play a fun game of "Run from the Dragon."
- *Goggles:* Even if you don't go swimming, you probably have some relatives who spit when they talk.
- *Flashlight:* You never know when you'll have to convince drunken relatives that there's a UFO flying overhead.
- *Pocket knife:* If that nephew who's been terrorizing your daughter accidentally ties his swimsuit drawstring in too many knots, do him a favor by severing the string completely. He can't throw rocks at your daughter if he has to hold his pants up.
- *Secret stash of alcohol:* You may need to trade for beaver pelts or hamburger buns with other campsites. Money is useless at Copter-Rescue State Park, but firewater means business.

Family Camping Danger Signs

When you're out in the woods, you must remain alert for snakes, bears, and family meltdowns. Here are just a few signs that you should immediately move your campsite to the Hyatt:

- You hear someone say, "Most bears are friendly and just want you to run from them so they can get a little exercise."
- You hear a kid cry, "Mommy, Daddy dropped my hot dog in the dirt but he's making me eat it." To which you hear the mom yell, "Shut up and eat your dirty hot dog! There are kids in China who only wish their factory cafeteria served hot dogs!"
- You catch two cousins arguing over which makes a better campfire, gasoline, or kerosene.
- Someone asks where the bathroom is, and the others point to the lake where you've spent the past two days swimming.

Fun Activities

These activities are sure to keep you from thinking about how comfortable you'd be sleeping in your own bed, and not on a pile of tree roots:

- *Shoe melting contests:* The first to melt the sole completely off of a shoe by the heat of the campfire gets an extra ration of s'mores.
- *Does this toy float or sink to the bottom of the lake (for kids)?* Your parents probably spent a lot of money on your toys, so don't you owe it to them to see which ones can float and which will be forever lost at the bottom of Lake Mercury? The winner has toys to play with the next day. The loser has a collection of favorite twigs.
- *Oldest-sleeping-bag contest:* Whoever has shunned modern sleeping-bag technology for those Civil War–era bags that look like

someone sewed together two blankets stolen from a Motel 6 knows what camping is really about. The person with the oldest, most decrepit sleeping bag is awarded a piece of chocolate that used to have ants on it till someone washed it in the lake.

■ *Find the restrooms at night:* Walking through a dark, spooky forest with a full bladder is made even more fun if you try to ambush the one for whom nature has called and scare the you-know-what out of them. The winner doesn't need an excuse for why they're wearing a swimsuit the next day.

FAMILY CAMPING DOS AND DON'TS

A few things we should or shouldn't do:

Do: Cook over an open campfire. Every dinner should begin with a course of carcinogen-flavored hamburgers cut fresh off the ground-beef tube, just like in olden times. Nothing beats the rich, smoky flavor of carbon monoxide.

Don't: Fully cook your meat. Food-borne illness is all part of the "roughing it" experience.

Do: Have a harmonica on you at all times. There is nothing like the sound of hobo music to make camping feel like being homeless.

Don't: Sing "Kumbaya." For that matter, avoid songs about calamine lotion and looking over your dead dog Rover. In fact, don't sing at all. The last time a family sang together, it was the Jackson 5; and we all know how that turned out.

Do: Go on day hikes. It's the best way to catch lizards and disturb the local flora and fauna.

Don't: Go on night hikes, unless you've got a campsite wager on who can get the most mosquito bites without contracting a virus.

Aren't we All Just a Bunch of Happy Campers?

See, it won't be so bad. Now go get a Frisbee and see how deep in the forest you can toss it before your nephew no longer wants to play!

Survival Tips

1. At least when you're camping, you can carry lots of knives. Just *try* to have that much fun at parent-teacher night.

2. Play lots of fun games, like Which In-Law Is the Most Allergic to Poison Oak? It will provide a rich, bonding experience that won't go away for three to four weeks.

chapter 30

WHITE TRASH VS. WHITE COLLAR
(GETTING TOGETHER WITH THE "OTHER" SIDE OF THE FAMILY)

Wealth is the ability to fully experience life.

· HENRY DAVID THOREAU ·

. . . Then I suppose if you're middle class, you've only got the ability to experience the parts of life they sell at Wal-Mart.

When you were a kid, it didn't seem like there was any real difference between the two main sides of the family. You can't recall any differences in the cars they drove, the houses they lived in, or the language they used to curse out park rangers for telling them they can't start a garbage fire (even though they said that they're Native American). All you remember is how you and your cousin would braid each other's hair and practice kissing boys on each other. It never occurred to you that while she was the first in her class to develop an economic growth model for predicting sales of *Tiger Beat* magazine, you were the first in yours to develop breasts. All you remember is that she was jealous that you had a boyfriend before she had a reason to run to the nurse's office during class.

Twenty-five years later, you live on tips from your job at an inner-city Denny's, while she's head of that company that recruits high school marching bands to sell magazine subscriptions to pay for their trips to Disneyland. She's about to marry a chiropractor who's become a minor celebrity in her hometown because of running TV commercials telling everyone that their backs hurt. You're on your third marriage, but this one will work because you're both Capricorns.

And now you two will be bringing your families together for a reunion. You have very different lifestyles and, if you aren't careful, you may say something to make the other side of the family feel awkward.

Let's review some things both sides of the family should avoid mentioning so as to have a comfortable reunion:

WE'RE OUT OF KETCHUP, BETTER HEAD DOWN TO BURGER KING

If you're from the side of the family who thinks that tennis bracelets are woven from broken racquet strings, here are a few examples of things you don't want to say around your rich relatives:

- *"I can't wait to buy a new superabsorbent mop at this year's county fair."* There are two problems with this comment. First, showing excitement about a fair tells someone that your life is built around funnel cakes, deep-fried candy bars, and airbrushed Raiders blankets. To your well-off family, this sounds like the adult equivalent of, "The ice-cream man's coming, the ice-cream man's coming." Why don't you just ask your relatives for a dollar and promise not to ruin your appetite? Your second mistake is the mop. Wanting to clean your home is a good sign, but your life must revolve around more than advancements in mop absorption. I don't care how charming the guy with the English accent and headset microphone is—it's still just a mop. Isn't there something better to be excited about than cutting five minutes off your daily ritual of removing Kool-Aid stains and cemented Cheerios from the linoleum?

■ *"By watch the news, do you mean* Entertainment Tonight?*"* Chances are, your well-to-do relatives like the same entertainment you do. The only difference is, they don't admit it. You should do the same, or risk being the answer to the question uttered by every disappointed channel surfer: "Who watches this crap?" More than anything you want to avoid a relative's having to say some polite dodge, you know, one of those, "Oh yeah, I think my kids watch that." Everybody loves video clips of babies kicking their dads in the nuts, but they keep it to themselves.

■ *"I eat at McDonald's because there is a chance I could scratch-and-win a million dollars."* We all like winning money, but admitting you only eat at places where there is a chance of a jackpot sends the wrong message. Your well-off aunt may worry that you won't touch her famous lemon bars unless she tells you one of them contains her missing diamond earrings.

So I Said, "If that's Brie, My Name Is Reginald Denny."

Now let's look at a few examples of what not to say to avoid offending the trailer trash:

■ *"Which Hawaiian Island is your favorite?"* Unless the more modest side of the family has won that McDonald's million-dollar sweepstakes, chances are, they've only seen Hawaii in reruns of

Magnum P.I. If you must discuss your travels, stick to talking about the hotel you stayed in. That way, the "other" relatives can respond with, "Yeah, one time I sprang for a Best Western. It was amazing! They had apples available twenty-four hours a day. It was like renting a room in an orchard!"

■ *"My Sonicare gets my teeth so clean, you can eat off them."* Chances are, the last time your other relatives got a new toothbrush, the dentist gave it to them. Not everyone can afford an eighty-dollar toothbrush. And talking about toothbrushes may make them self-conscious about their "sunshiny" smiles (and by *sunshiny*, we mean *yellow*). In general, don't talk about any recent purchases unless it's something like, "I bought a ferret cage off eBay for fifteen bucks!" That's something they can appreciate.

■ *"Want to see pictures from the triathlon I ran last week?"* It's not that those of lesser means can't afford to do triathlons, it just cuts into their TV time. Talking about proactive sports hobbies is bad on two levels: First, you are rubbing your healthy lifestyle right in their faces. Why don't you just ask, "Guess how much lower my resting heart rate is than yours?" Second, people of lesser means rarely participate in triathlons. If they live near water, it's little more than a soup of mob bodies and PCBs; and running down those roads with numbers written on your legs will probably get you mistaken for some new gang invading the turf. That triathlon could very quickly become a biathlon.

BONDING

Now that you're clear on what not to say, let's discuss a fun way to bond with your "other" relatives, so you can learn about each other. This is a questions game, in which you ask the other side of the family what something is.

For example, the well-off side of the family can ask, "What's a 401(k)?" To which the other side of the family may reply, "Isn't that a gun popular among gangs?" You reply, "No. You're thinking of an AK-47." Then explain it in terms they'll understand: "A 401(k) is like the place where you hide your beer money, except that you can't buy any beer with it till you're fifty-nine and a half."

Next, it's the other side of the family's turn. They can ask, "What's Moneytree?" You might reply, "Isn't that a tree criminals hollow out so they have a place to stash their money?" They can reply, "No. Moneytree is like a bank, except instead of offering home loans, they offer drug-habit and back-rent loans."

You can play the game as long as you want, or until everyone decides to stop and just braid each other's hair.

GIVE FROM THE HEART—OR WHEREVER YOU KEEP YOUR MONEY

No matter what your economic situation, remember that family is family. Both sides need each other. The more modest side can remind the other that they are just a few bad decisions away from spending the rest of their lives being the "Okay, *go!*" guy at the top of the waterslide. And the more modest family can recognize that with a little night school, they could probably move into a neighborhood that the police don't have codenames for.

SURVIVAL TIPS

1. If you are well-off, don't appear snobbish to the other side of the family by talking about how your Lexus can park itself. You may be talking to someone who works as a valet.

2. If you pay attention, you'll notice similarities between each side of the family. For example, the only difference between a monogrammed belt buckle and a monogrammed cardigan is the place where someone who wants to know your initials has to look.

3. They say that the major difference in people of different means is their ability to delay gratification. Unfortunately, most poor people think delayed gratification means waiting till your parents fall asleep on the other side of the trailer before you and your boyfriend can have sex.

chapter 31

RED- AND BLUE-STATERS
(WHAT TO DO WHEN THE "TWO AMERICAS" SHOW UP AT THE SAME FAMILY REUNION)

Politics make strange bedfellows.

· CHARLES DUDLEY WARNER ·

. . . If politics among family members also makes strange bedfellows, your reunion is probably being held in the Appalachian Mountains.

Every year, family reunions bring together our conservative and liberal relatives for a time-honored tradition of eating barbeque and accusing the "other side" of destroying America. But just because we've got relatives from "red" and "blue" states with differing political views doesn't mean our family gathering will turn into a joint session of Congress. These events *can* be peaceful. Our family members *can* put aside their differences and focus on common interests, like keeping the uncle everyone refuses to let babysit from taking the kids on a nature walk.

It can be quite disturbing to witness our "red" and "blue" relatives gearing up to stab each other during a debate about what causes violence in America. That is, unless you understand how "red" and "blue" relatives are different, how they ended up in the same family, what to watch for to avoid getting sucked into a political argument, and how to stop a fight before the kids overhear enough adult words to make their "What I learned this summer" essays sound like an episode of *The Sopranos*.

RED- AND BLUE-STATERS 101

Let's begin by looking at some little-known facts about red- and blue-staters: Did you know conservative red-staters have six toes on each foot? It's true. They use the extra toe to press harder on the gas pedals of their environment-destroying, fossil fuel–guzzling SUVs. Red-staters also have an extra set of protective eyelids they can close while hunting or watching the news.

Did you know liberal blue-staters also have an extra muscle in their forehead that allows them to roll their eyes two centimeters higher than everyone else? It's true. And blue-staters sigh an octave higher than most people. Blue-staters also read from top to bottom, so as not to offend Chinese people; red-staters consider reading to be one of the black arts. They will only put their eyes to a document if it's an appropriation of wetlands or a bill to make Birkenstocks illegal.

Blue-staters are fine with having Spanish as a second national language, because they have no cultural identity. Red-staters claim that the country already has a second national language: motor-engine revving. When it comes to entertainment, blue-staters will watch anything, so long as it's based on a vial of tears found in an immigrant's basement. Red-staters will also watch anything, provided that it features a robot, nuclear attack, or crime-fighting aliens.

Red- and blue-staters are so different, it's amazing they can live in the same country, let alone share a beach house one week a year. Just how in the heck did such different people come to be in the same family?

YEAH, THAT'S MY COUSIN . . . WE DON'T KNOW WHAT HAPPENED

There are two main ways in which families get both "red" and "blue" representatives:

1. *A child rebels against her parents:* Those greasy, patchouli-stinking hippie parents were only helpful on crafts day in school (when your teacher was quite amazed with your ability to turn a milk carton into a bong). You loved them, but also resented that they never understood your desire to be the largest paper manufacturer in China. So you attended the University of Washington on a deforestation scholarship and learned business, and now, when your parents roll a joint, they do it on paper you made. You've become the person your parents protested against. They'd give you a hard time about clear-cutting South America, but they're way too high.

2. *A person marries into the enemy (a.k.a. the Greg and Dharma Initiative):* Ever since you ran your first lemonade stand and developed a program that allowed kids without twenty-five cents to apply for lemonade stamps, your parents have been worried that you might become a political defector. Your family's so Republican that they never fed the dog—believing that the free market would produce a business to take care of Fido (unfortunately, that business was the Pawsoleum). And you thought you were a staunch conservative as well, until you went to college and met Cliff—a boy so liberal that be believed corporations

should pay for bestiality partners' health benefits/vet bills. Before you knew it, you were meeting his parents, wearing hemp undergarments, and insisting that your wedding cake be in the shape of Michael Moore.

IDIOTS WHO TALK POLITICS

Occasionally we'll become the target of a relative who insists on turning the family reunion into a demonstration of how much "knowledge" eight years of student loans buys, or how listening to fifteen hours of talk radio per week has somehow turned a truck-driving uncle into a policy wonk.

Here are some of the common politically minded (the term being used loosely) relatives to watch out for:

- *The PAVs (Political Assault Vehicles):* These people use politics to attack you, and make you feel like a bad or irresponsible person: "Are you *really* going to shop at a supermarket that refuses to support its grocery-checkers' union? Why don't you just eat a baby!!"
- *Volunteeristas:* These people think that getting personally involved would give your life the same meaning it gave them: "You know, I think you'd really learn a lot if you joined our cell, er, I mean our organization. We could really use your help setting fire to university greenhouses."
- *Coalition of the whining:* These people rope you into a political discussion so you can form a majority party against another member of the family: "Your Aunt Mabel believes that it's OK to murder someone if he takes your parking space. You and I should try to talk some sense into her."

HOW TO DEFEND YOURSELF FROM AN "IDIOT WHO TALKS POLITICS"

With a little thoughtfulness, escaping a political argument is as easy as pie. Let's say one of your aunts is part of that protesting-grannies group. She knows you bought an SUV. You only got it because you've got a few kids and needed the space to haul around their lawn mower–powered go-carts and your collection of gas-guzzling leaf blowers.

She'll ask something like, "Do you know how much warmer you're making the atmosphere with that gigantic truck you drive?"

Possible responses:
If you say, "No, I don't," you're in for a lecture.
If you say, "I don't care," you're in for a lecture and maybe a fight.

If you and she are alone:
In this situation, you can either mock: "Not my car! My car is made of compressed tea leaves and it runs on prayers from the Dalai Lama."

Or crap on the comment: "Do you know how much warmer you're making that ogling old man on the park bench?"

If in a group:
If she attacks your vehicle while everyone's sitting around the picnic bench together, you've got a few options: (1) Bring in other victims: "My car actually gets twenty-five miles per gallon. Isn't that about what your car gets, Grammy Nickels?" Now she isn't just attacking you, but also dear Grammy Nickels.

Or, (2) mock her attack: "And do you know what the funny thing is? I accidentally hit an endangered panda while driving it the other day. It cracked my engine casing and oil spilled everywhere. It would've stained the road but, fortunately, there was a lake at the bottom of the street and the oil drained right in. Good thing, or it could've been quite a mess." This should hopefully elicit laughter from the other family members who didn't want a political discussion to begin with. Your "idiot who talks politics" should stay silent, at least until dessert is served.

You Down with O.P.P. (Other People's Politics)

If you aren't the target of the relative's attack, you have the ability to put an end to a political argument. However, if the family reunion's a little slow, sometimes it's fun to watch your sister-in-law call your husband a freak because he insists that you can solve world hunger by opening more McDonald's. Also, if most of your family is feverishly debating the cause of obesity in America (probably a segue from the McDonald's comment), no one will notice if you eat the last two slices of apple pie.

But if you decide that you'd like to quell the political uprising at the picnic table, here are some tips:

- ■ *Find a common enemy.* In fact, if Martians ever invade Earth to steal our water, it will probably be the first time the reds and blues will agree on an immigration policy. Since that's at least a year or two away from actually happening, try saying something like, "I think we can all agree that despite our differences, no one wants to get a staph infection."
- ■ *Fill arguing mouths with dessert.* It's hard to argue when Uncle Frank's famous "diabetes disk" triple-sugar cookies are being shoved down your throat.
- ■ *Cry.* Yes, when in doubt, there is nothing like a host bursting into tears to trump arguing family members. In general, anytime a family gathering gets out of hand, crying like a baby can be

thought of as hitting the red emergency button. The only difference is that instead of the police showing up, your single aunt runs over to smother you in one of her famous "I need a boyfriend" hugs.

I TOLD YOU I WAS RIGHT

See? All our fears of a giant political debate at this year's family reunion were for naught. With just a little understanding and preparation, our liberal and conservative relatives will get along so well, you'd think they were family.

SURVIVAL TIPS

1. Watch out for historical facts. Historical facts dropped into conversation are the Trojan horses of political discussions. If someone asks, "Do you know who *really* invented Persian rugs?" and his T-shirt has an image of Louis Farrakhan, it's best to pretend that you hear one of your kids crying at the bottom of a slide.

2. Mixed-politics marriages are just like mixed-race marriages, except your new "red" cousins won't try to scare you by driving you through their neighborhood.

3. When you're trying to stop a political discussion, a great technique is to cry. If you're a man, the blue-staters will think that you're brave for crying, and the red-staters will think that you've got that Chevy "Like a Rock" TV jingle stuck in your head, and have finally been overcome by its patriotic overtones.

chapter 32

THE JAWS OF LIFE
(WHAT TO SAY TO AVOID YOUR CRAZY-ASS UNCLE'S DIATRIBE ABOUT HOW PEOPLE USED TO BE FRIENDLIER OR WHATEVER)

What you talkin' about, Willis?

· ARNOLD DRUMMOND FROM DIFF'RENT STROKES ·

. . . I'm talkin' about something really inappropriate, boring, or irritating. What can you do to stop me?

Everyone has been cornered by a relative who won't let you go swimming until he's told you all he knows about Amsterdam's sex-trade industry. There's always some family member who lights up at the opportunity to tell you an inappropriate joke, share how he's taught himself to speed-read, or otherwise drag you into a conversation that makes you feel like that cat who's constantly trying to squeeze away from Pepe Le Peu. Well, fear not the relative with a lame, disgusting, or weird story! Here's a list of clever comebacks you can use when the conversation becomes a chat room you need to log out of:

■ *"Hey, where are the kids?"* Say this anytime someone's about to spend three hours telling you about his backpacking trip through Guam. This line is a "Get out of a Long, Boring-Ass Story Free" card. The threat of a two-year-old swallowing a knife always trumps hearing about how big a frog Uncle Frankie saw on vacation.

■ *"Well, I respect your passion."* This is what you say to any family member who insists on trying to convince you to give up wearing fur, eating meat, or bathing. It's a way of politely saying, "I think you're an idiot, but I still like you."

■ *"I completely agree."* The key to using this one is saying, "I completely agree," the minute they start talking. Now they can't discuss the issue with you. You have already told them you think exactly as they do. There's nothing to discuss. And if you want to get fancy, you can follow your "I completely agree" with, "Hey, where are the kids?"

■ *"Hold that thought; I'll be right back."* You have no intention of coming back, but this is a great thing to say if this is the third or fourth time you've had to use the Jaws of Life. If "Hey, where are the kids?" and "I completely agree" haven't encouraged this relative to go help Grandpa with the barbeque, this straight-up ditch should do the trick.

■ *"You should meet my friend Sharon, she's totally into boring shit as well."* Not the most subtle response, but great for a cousin or in-law who doesn't seem to get how uninterested you are in hearing how they make homemade aphid repellant.

■ *"Someone wanted your help with something over by the picnic tables."* This is for the sad-sack relative who is talking to you so they have someone to stand next to. This brush-off needs to be sensitive and effective, so telling them someone *needs* them is much better than saying, "Don't you have some other cousin who's drunk enough to pretend they want to hear your synopsis of *Death of a Salesman*?"

Chances are that whenever they make it over to the picnic tables and ask, "Cousin Julie says someone here needs my help?" they will also show the same sensitivity you did and say, "I think she meant someone needed your help by the fire pit."

■ *"Oh yeah, I've known that for a while now."* The target of this comeback is the relative who gives you tidbits of surprising information so you'll somehow mistake her having an interesting story for being an interesting person. In order to discourage her desire to let you know that Coca-Cola is owned by the Mormons and that Jell-O is made with pig hooves, you've got to make sure that whatever proxy for "interesting" she's throwing at you is old news. You can even flip the script by replying, *"Everyone* knows that," to suggest that not only isn't she breaking news that zebras aren't horses, she may in fact be the last person on Earth to know this.

■ "_____" (*The awkward silence response*). If a wily relative is trying to spark up a conversation with you around a group of people, one of the best covers is simply to pretend you didn't hear them. They may blurt out, "You'll never guess who just got her tubes tied?" Just stand with your eyes focused onto something else as though your head is in another dimension. Let their question or comment hang in the air like the branch of a dead sycamore. If they repeat the question, just calmly pretend to be part of another conversation, or lost in your own thoughts. If they say your name, like, "Hey, Bettie, guess whose factory shut its doors?" Try to cut them off midsentence by talking to someone else. Then you can turn back, and say, "Oh, what was that?"

■ *"We'll send you pictures."* Occasionally, you can make the mistake of telling the wrong relative about something you've recently done. Rather than a normal level of polite interest, these people become obsessed with every little detail of your story. Either they want you to reciprocate interest by saying, "Enough about me. Now I want to hear about how you put a bird net over your cherry tree," or they are truly interested in your story. Regardless, if you're no longer interested in telling them about your road trip through Texas, saying that you'll send pictures is a great solution. It sounds to them like you're saying, "Well, if you're really that interested, let me show you actual images from the trip"—but what you're really communicating is, "Let me just send you the pictures so I don't have to keep talking to you."

You were Saying?

These Jaws of Life are a set of tools no family reunion-goers should be without. With these phrases at your disposal, even that one relative who keeps asking you to feel his biceps will be no match for your training. If you can't recall any relative bothering you with an annoying or inappropriate conversation, then ask your other relatives if anyone's done that to them. Chances are they'll say, "Grandpa wants your help by the fire pit."

SURVIVAL TIPS

1. The art of nodding your head: to feign interest, be sure to give one to one and a half "uh-huh's" per head-nod. Otherwise it just looks like you're about to sneeze.

2. If you want to pretend to get a call on your cell phone, it's recommended that before the conversation even begins, you say, "Not to be rude, but I'm expecting an important call." Then if the conversation begins to take a turn for the weird, and you whip out your phone, it'll practically be a Pavlovian cue for him to walk away.

3. Although it's not a way to escape a conversation, pretending to have a busted toe is a great excuse for getting out of Ultimate Frisbee, croquet, or any other half-sport you won't condescend to play. If anyone asks why you're not limping on your fake broken toe, tell them you're demonstrating bravery and leadership.

PART

xI

MY DADDY LIVES WITH THE CLEANING LADY NOW

(HOW TO HANDLE DIVORCES AND FAMILY SHIFTS)

chapter 33

SO, WHERE DID YOU MEET MY DADDY
(AND DO A LOT OF WHORES HANG OUT THERE)?

I love being a single mom. But it's definitely different when you're dating.

· BROOKE BURNS ·

. . . The biggest difference being that if a guy wants to score a home run with me, he's got to wait for my little third-base coach to wave him in.

You have a right to be happy. And following a divorce, you have a right to go out there and meet that special someone who, unlike your ex, doesn't think foreplay is having dinner before seeing *A Streetcar Named Desire.*

However, your family may not see your side of things. If you've got young children, they'll be going through as much emotional turmoil as you. But they don't have an outlet for their grief. You can go out and have rebound sex, but a young kid can't pick up a new mother at a Chuck E. Cheese's singles night and go for an ice-cream quickie.

Even adult children will need some time for the adjustment. Nothing's more awkward than seeing your dad hook up with that real-estate lady who always used to leave pumpkins on the doorstep come Halloween. Sure, her face looked attractive plastered across a bus-station backstop, but you never thought it'd inspire him to put his house on the market just to meet her. This new relationship forces you to consider the possibility that your parent is not the asexual caregiver you knew in your youth. He's a flesh-and-blood person with needs that must be satisfied. Yuck!

If you're a parent, then no matter what your family dynamic, you must prepare if you want to have a successful transition back into the dating scene.

You Remember Bill, Mommy's Friend from Work?

Young children can have a tough time when you start dating again—unless you explain your activities in terms that they can understand and support. Here are some examples that both men and women can follow to help explain dating to young kids:

We don't like the babysitter. Why can't Mommy come over and babysit?
"Mommy's got a magical bracelet around her ankle that won't let her leave her apartment. She'd love to babysit, but if she gets within five hundred yards of the house, the police are going to babysit *her*—for twelve to eighteen months."

Why do you have to go out tonight, Mommy?
"You have friends at school, right? Well, Mommy also needs friends she can play with—she can't play with herself forever."

Do you love your new friend more than Mommy?

"I'm always going to love your mommy. But Elaine has something she doesn't—the ability to regulate her serotonin levels."

Why did Elaine spend the night?

"We had a sleepover party. And just like your sleepover parties, it began by watching a few movies. We also made one."

An Eye For an Eye, a Tooth For a Tot

While the above responses will, no doubt, satisfy a child's every curiosity about your new dating life, there will still be the occasional evening that he tries to sabotage. If you thought it was annoying to be cock-blocked by a college roommate, wait until you're out to dinner and get a call informing you that your son has set fire to the babysitter (although in his defense, she was complaining that she was cold). When your child does these things, don't get angry. You can't really blame him for these kinds of actions. Ruining your life is just part of his adjustment process.

But how do you handle it when a child sabotages your date? You can't crush the uprising with extreme punishment. Remember the mistake made by being too harsh to Germany following World War One? Before you know it, your son will emerge as a brutal dictator, and blame your two cats for all the family's problems. Unless you want to notice unused litter and a missing shoebox, you'd better take it easy on Junior. And you certainly don't want to bribe your son with toys. This teaches him that you can acquire things by protesting— and will no doubt lead to an exciting career as a rent-a-mob picketer.

If your child ruins one of your dates, the only thing you can do is ruin one of his. When one of his freckle-faced friends rings the doorbell, inquiring if your son can play, lose your shit. Throw a shrieking,

embarrassing temper tantrum that'll make your child wonder if his
mom's been replaced by that severe-ADD kid from school who cries
and hurls potted plants every time he has to take a standardized test.
Then, when his friend leaves in horror, turn to your son and say, "You
see? You don't like it when I ruin *your* playtime, do you?" Now he
understands the pain he causes you when he ruins your dates. In fact,
the next time *your* boyfriend comes over, your son will be so polite, he
probably won't even come out of his room.

WOULD DADDY'S NEW FRIEND LIKE TO STAY FOR DINNER?

Unlike with young kids, you won't have to do much explaining to
your adult children regarding why you're dating again (and with
modern ED medications, you don't have to explain how). But there
are a few key areas to understand and consider:

- *We're just friends (with benefits . . . through AARP):* When you first
  mention your new love interest, begin by referring to her as your
  "friend." A friend is someone with whom you go bowling, not a
  person who'll grab your knee under the dinner table, then whisper in your ear that she'd like to see your home's bonus room.
  Of course, everyone knows that you two are more than chums.
  But it's a lot easier on your family to tell them about your new
  "buddy," than explain to them that you're now hot-n-heavy with
  the real estate queen of Kirkland—whose turn-ons include doing
  it in her clients' empty homes.
- *You should meet her—you'll love her:* Next, if your kids live nearby,
  try to arrange for an introduction over a casual lunch or dinner.
  Avoid having the first meeting during Christmas or a major family event. Tensions are usually high enough during the holidays,
  without your kids wondering why some whore is running around

in their mom's apron. However, if you must introduce your new love during a holiday, make sure you both give separate presents. The situation will be plenty awkward without your kids having to open Christmas cards from "Dad and Shelly."

■ *I'm not your real mommy:* Your ex, their mother, was a gregarious, bubbly blonde who was such a devout believer in the healing power of crystals that she was once thrown out of a hospital for gluing amethyst shards to a cystic fibrosis patient. But your new girlfriend is a slinky, bookish brunette who becomes sexually aroused every time you use the word *erudite.* She refers to crystals as "don't think for yourself" rocks, and the only thing she and your ex have in common is that they're inexplicably attracted to you.

To your kids, it's actually easier if they see you with someone unlike their mother. It's understandable to need a new companion. However, hooking up with another bubbly blonde, with the only difference being that her "bubbles" are twenty years younger, just makes you appear horny and lecherous. That isn't a good enough reason to send their mother trolling for a new dude on Craigslist—with five topaz amulets over her heart.

I Said, "Go To Bed!"

No matter what, it'll simply take time for your kids to accept your new love interest. And for those of you with younger children, just be patient. Before you know it, they'll address your new boyfriend (or girlfriend) with such politeness and respect that it may actually help your hook-up. Nothing's cuter than your little one's saying, "I've cleaned my room, so I think I'll just go to bed. See you two kids in the morning."

SURVIVAL TIPS

1. Tell young kids that your having a new boyfriend is just like their having a new soccer coach. This way, if you two break up after a year, they'll just think the season's ended.

2. Scientific fact: When it comes to dating, a single mother develops a predatory streak that would make a shark seem like Mother Teresa.

3. No matter how serious your new relationship, be prepared for one of your kids to give you the "use a condom" speech as a bit of fun revenge for the one you gave him years ago. Just resist the temptation to reply, "If only I'd taken that advice thirty years ago, I wouldn't have to sit here and listen to you lecture me."

chapter 34

VISITATION RITES
(SEEING FAMILY AFTER A DIVORCE)

Attitudes are more important than facts.

· GEORGE MACDONALD ·

. . . Such as the "bald is beautiful" attitude is more important than the fact that this is only true among babies and basketball stars.

Families are like NASCAR fans—they love visiting, but mostly to see you crash. That means the first time you visit family after a divorce, you can expect them to consider your story regarding "what happened" to be part of the festivities. Somewhere between "Jingle Bells" and "Frosty the Snowman," they're going to want you to do an a cappella version of "Rudolf the Absentee Father." The problem, of course, is that rehashing the details of your divorce is about as high on your list as giving a slideshow presentation of your yeast infection (at least it wouldn't be the same old boring pictures of the Grand Canyon).

To avoid having your recent breakup ruin your family visit, you must manage two key areas: your appearance and your attitude.

wow, You Look GRRRREAT!!
(THE WOMAN'S APPEARANCE)

Relatives will consider how you look to be a sign of how you're handling the breakup. You want to appear as though you aren't just surviving; you're thriving! You need to show up looking hotter and younger than you've looked in years.

Begin by turning yourself into a bleach blonde (if you've already got blond hair, then dye your locks Queen Elizabeth red). Then make your hair so big that should you walk through a zoo, the lion tamer will strike your ass with a whip and demand that you climb onto a barrel. It's highly recommended that you update your wardrobe to include no fewer than three tiger-striped, skintight pants, and four leopard-spotted blouses. But don't buy your feline-themed attire until you've dropped at least ten pounds. If you're already thin, stop eating for a few weeks (no longer than a month—just to stay healthy) and go for that emaciated supermodel look.

Your family was expecting a dumpy old divorcee, but you'll arrive as a cougar ready to pounce. And pounce you should. If there are any available men at the family gathering (who, except in the most desperate cases, are not relations), be sure to hit on them. Of course, it may piss off whoever brought them. So what? It's not your fault you look hot.

ARR, YE NEW POTENTIAL MATIE
(THE MAN'S APPEARANCE)

For men to escape the same scrutiny that faces their female counterparts, they must choose from one of two pirate-inspired looks. If you're a newly single, balding buccaneer, then you must shave your head and pierce one or both of your ears—depending on how much (and what type of) booty you plan on plundering. With one trip to the barber shop, you'll go from a man whose attractiveness to the opposite sex is receding at the same rate as his hairline, to emanating a virile, professional-athlete potency.

If you've still got a full head of hair, you must then grow it long. Even if you're an accountant, or hold some other office job where a conservative look is the norm, you must appear as though you're that mysterious horse trainer from the dog-eared pages of romance novels. This tells your family that you're a rebel, and that you aren't afraid of looking like some old dude who's decided to grow his hair long.

Also, it's rare that an overweight pirate would sail the seven seas. So lose those twenty pounds you use to keep temptation from the minds of your female co-workers. You're now a swashbuckler, so make sure you can also be a belt buckler.

However, if you absolutely can't drop your marriage weight, then adorn yourself with sparkling gold necklaces, bracelets, and a ring on every finger—one of which must be from your high school gradua-tion. You'll be so shiny that onlookers will have to squint, and notice only a fraction of your true girth.

Now when you show up to this year's Christmas or family gath-ering, it won't appear as though you've lost your wife and kids, but rather that you've rediscovered your machismo. Your family was thinking they'd have to buoy the spirits of a forty-year-old facing the daunting prospect of reentering the dating scene. Now they'll notice that you're so ready to be single again, you've even started wearing too much cologne.

DRIVE-BY SNOOTINGS
(THE WOMAN'S ATTITUDE)

Although your appearance will send a strong message that you're back and better than ever, it's inevitable that people will want to talk to you about the breakup. Other divorced relatives will no doubt offer support and invite you out with them, either to hunt for men at singles' bars or to get ice cream—depending on which they think will make a better companion (at least when you eat too much ice cream, you know it'll stick around for a while).

The problems arise when not-so-sympathetic relatives want to talk. You'll have some snooty female relative who'll want to "comfort" you by telling you how great *her* marriage is, and what she does to keep her dear Beauford from jumping ship (or their daughter's piano teacher). The right attitude will keep us from becoming a casualty of her drive-by "snooting." For example, if you get a condescending, "Awww. What happened?" just reply with something like, "He decided to become a gangsta rapper, and I refused to shake my ass in one of his music videos—so basically, we had creative differences." Your relative was probably hoping for one of the "We just grew apart" or "He met someone else" lines, so she could douse you with her Dr. Philistine advice. But what kind of response can you expect when you tell her that your husband, the dentist, now has gold teeth and bought his first gun—just in time for the MTV Video Music Awards? She'll respond by backing that ass up, away from you and back to Beauford, that's how.

DUDE LOOKS LIKE A BABY
(THE MAN'S ATTITUDE—OR LACK THEREOF)

Men must also cop the right attitude. But chances are, many of the women (and a few guys) in your family are going to think that you're the reason for the breakup. In fact, most women typically think divorces occur because the man was unfaithful, or emotionally distant, abrasive, and insensitive. No one knows where these broads get this crap. But so as not to appear as though you've transformed into some kind of cloven-hoofed, home-wrecking beast, your attitude must be that of the "softie."

Immediately upon arriving, approach the womenfolk and tell them how hurt you are by the breakup. Explain how your ex made fun of you for trying to listen to her feelings, hated it when you'd cook for her, and only spent time with the children when she wanted to drive in the carpool lane. If you want to throw a cherry on top, you can even tell them that she used to put cigarettes out on the kids' foreheads. Despite your love, you just couldn't have that kind of a mother raising your kids.

By explaining that it ended because she had the parenting skills of a Hells Angel, you'll go from bastard to victim. They'll see you as a great guy, and if they do talk to you about your personal life, it'll be to find out which of their friends you'd like to date.

And if you no longer want to talk about it, just pretend to be on the verge of tears. If you need to, think about how much money you lost betting on last year's Super Bowl. Unless he's trying to interrupt an argument (see Red- and Blue-Staters), a crying man is the equivalent of a person in medieval times running through the streets with open, pus-filled sores: it's hideous, and all one can do is hope that like a cat, he finds an abandoned building in which to die.

IT'S FOR THE BEST, RIGHT?

Divorce is tough enough without having to explain to the family why your kids now have a bunch of new, expensive toys that seem to be purchased directly from the "Where's Daddy?" winter catalogue. If both men and women take the time to manage their appearances and attitudes, the only concerns they'll have this holiday is where to buy a tiger-striped Santa hat; or how to politely tell women that they aren't Bruce Willis—even if it's already too late.

SURVIVAL TIPS

1. Recently divorced men must transform themselves into pirates. Either shave your head, or grow your hair long. You can even wear an eye patch. If family asks what happened to your eye, tell them you lost it in the divorce.

2. In order to impress your relatives with how liberated you've become since "he" left, be sure to make your contribution to the dinner conversation a discussion of Tantric sex and why it's always important to get a colonic before the third date.

3. If you do get roped into explaining why the divorce occurred, avoid repeating empty stock lines, such as, "Everything happens for a reason" or "It just wasn't meant to be." All people will be thinking is, "Yeah, I guess she just wasn't meant to be with a guy whose most meaningful conversations always began with, 'I'm hungry.'"

chapter 35

MOMMY'S NEW BOYFRIEND KEEPS SENDING ME OUT FOR PIZZA

(KIDS AND DIVORCE)

The family is a haven in a heartless world.

· ATTRIBUTED TO CHRISTOPHER LASCH ·

. . . And nowhere is this more beautifully displayed than during a custody dispute.

Your parents got divorced for one simple reason: they knew that you were ready to be an adult. If your dad thought that you needed more supervision, he wouldn't have been caught celebrating Secretary's Day by the private investigator your mom hired. He could tell that you'd grown tired of Saturday-morning cartoons and eating dinner as a family. You were ready to spend your time hanging out in front of liquor stores and playing "seven minutes in heaven" with high school kids.

I'M FOURTEEN, DAD. I'M NOT A KID ANYMORE

To step into the new shoes left to you in the divorce settlement, you must make a few changes in your life:

■ *Smoking:* Now that you're an adult, you're going to need to shed that youthful-looking baby skin. Nothing says, "I may look fourteen, but I'm a grownup!" like constantly puffing away on a pack-a-day habit. You should start smoking as soon as one of your parents moves out, so that by the time you graduate (or drop out of) high school, your complexion will have the tough, mature carapace of a construction worker.

■ *Clothes:* Old people are known to have poor circulation, and are therefore constantly cold. You're just as mature as any octogenarian, and can prove it by bundling yourself in a large, heat-absorbing, black trench coat and skintight, black jeans. When people see you, you won't just look like some poorly dressed quasi-orphan from a dysfunctional family. They'll think, "Wow, that kid must have the circulatory system of an eighty-year-old." You can also paint your fingernails black, and wear black lipstick (boy or girl), as that will also send the message that you're in desperate need of raising your body temperature.

■ *Choosing a mate:* If you're in your early teens, it's time to find someone to settle down with. Your parents have split up, and now it's time to create the stable relationship they couldn't. You may be new to this type of commitment, so here are a few pointers: Begin by signing a suicide pact with your boyfriend or girlfriend, stating that you two will be together forever, that you'll never change, and that if one of you dies or decides to go to community college, the other will do the same. Then start planning on how you'll make a living. But don't waste your time thinking about in-demand trades or professions. Be bold and figure out how many painted-rock paperweights you'd have to sell to afford a beach house in Santa Cruz. Also, start planning on what the two of you will do when you both turn eighteen. Where will you run away to? In which city will you become vagrants? Your future is too important not to consider these details ahead of time.

■ *Death metal or speed metal?* Occasionally, a parent may wake up and decide that she doesn't want you to become an adult just yet. In fact, she may try to impede your growth by attempting to become a parent again. To thwart her effort, become obsessed with some form of weird or disturbing music. Fortunately, there are a lot of bands that can help you send frightening messages to your parents, such as Life of Agony and Drowning Pool. It's highly recommended that upon buying these bands' albums, you commit their lyrics to memory, or scratch them into your skin with a rusty paperclip. This will empower you to answer a parent's plea to clean your room with, "Why? We're all going to die anyway. What does it matter?"

If you rarely see your father, you may want to become obsessed with music from Cher, Elton John, or vintage music from bands such as the Smiths or Echo and the Bunnymen. This will send the message to your dad that because of his decision to forgo attending your baseball games so that he could pursue becoming regional district director of the senior vice president of the territory chairman of marketing, operations, administration, and casual Fridays for the third largest touchless-flush toilet company in North America, you now play for the other team.

STOP TALKING TO ME LIKE I'M A KID

Now that you're an adult, you must accept one final responsibility: if you're the only one out of all your friends whose parents are divorced, then your house must be made available for illicit after-school activities. Everyone else's parents probably get home before eight P.M. (their mothers don't have to hit the pub in search of new hubbies). You're now an important part of the juvenile ecosystem—except, unlike protected wetlands, people come over to your house to *get* polluted.

SURVIVAL TIPS

1. Athletic kids of recently divorced parents may also find it constructive to join a fight club, or engage in extreme backyard wrestling. Not only will this prepare you for future alcohol-induced altercations, but these activities teach life skills such as how to take a punch, and what it feels like to be knocked unconscious by a folding chair.

2. The key to a good, child-of-divorced-parents breakfast is that it must be so bad for you, it makes your loser friends whose parents force them to eat cereal and eggs, jealous. You may no longer have parental supervision, but who cares when you can start the day with a bag of pork rinds and a Coke.

×II

OVER MY DEAD BODY

(SURVIVING FUNERALS)

chapter 36

FUNERAL STORIES THAT HONOR THE DEAD

A funeral eulogy is a belated plea for the
defense delivered after the evidence is all in.

· IRVIN S. COBB ·

. . . And if it's your family doing the talking,
you'd better hope for a mistrial.

When a loved one passes away, the proper thing to do is to remember him fondly—no matter what. This can be a tough task. When we must eulogize or share a story about a deceased relative, some of us face a real challenge: What if our loved one was a douche bag? What do we say when called upon to remember relatives we loved, but who may not have been the nicest or most normal people in the world? Even if they weren't terrible individuals, they may have been weird, or had questionable circumstances surrounding their demise. How do we appropriately and lovingly honor these people? You don't want to lie, yet you want to be positive.

OSAMA BELIEVED IN FLYING HIGH, REGARDLESS OF OBSTACLES

If you search your heart, you'll find the correct way to express yourself about even the worst relative. Here are some examples of how to turn a negative reality into a positive remembrance:

Evil: Grandpa Ferris was an alcoholic who beat his kids.

Inspiring: Grandpa Ferris was a man of high spirits who believed in the school of hard knocks.

Despicable: Great-Aunt Suzie was a two-timing whore.

Admirable: Great-Aunt Suzie couldn't get enough out of life.

Disturbing: Uncle David was killed by his wife to collect an insurance settlement.

Noble: Uncle David will be remembered by his family as the ultimate provider.

Unconscionable: Uncle Bill was a bastard who cheated his own brothers in business.

Grounded: Uncle Bill believed a good family is all the wealth one needs.

Unpatriotic: Cousin Sam became confused, changed his name to Saddam, flew to Iraq, and is currently in the company of seventy-two virgins.

Uplifting: Cousin Sam thought life was a blast.

Strange: Great-Aunt Karen often used road kill to make stews and pot pies.

Spiritual: Great-Aunt Karen believed every animal had its place in this world (and often, that place was inside each of us).

I Didn't Know Anyone Like Him

Sometimes, you may be called upon to share an anecdote about a deceased relative you barely knew. Of course, you want the entire family to recognize what a special relationship you had with Grandpa What's-His-Face, so here are a few tips on how to pull this off:

- *I'm so sorry for your loss:* When you see someone crying at a funeral, it means either that he or she was very close to the deceased, or has to foot the bill for the solid mahogany casket. When you arrive, you need to seek these people out and ask, "What's your fondest memory of Grandpa What's-His-Face?" This will give you the information necessary to formulate your own story. For example, if she says, "He had such an adventurous spirit," you know that you can say something like, "I remember when Grandpa jumped his motorcycle over a burning bus," confident that it will sound completely realistic.

- *A game of one-on-one:* When remembering a relative you barely knew, make sure your story refers to a time when just the two of you were together. Avoid talking about Thanksgivings, family reunions, or other times when there could've been witnesses to discredit your story. Good examples would be: "I remember when Grandpa showed me his collection of illegal firearms" or "I remember when Grandpa taught me how to run a credit-card scam." Then, if you want, you can offer to help pay for part of the wake, handing the widow a shiny new Visa card.

He Was a Dear, Dear Man

No matter what kind of person he was, or how well you knew him, you should have no problem honoring his memory and simultaneously portraying a bereaved relative. Remember, funerals are a time to celebrate the life of one of your own. Just as Hollywood movies will often add colorful details to biographies, you should also feel free to brighten up the memory of a less-than-saintly relative—even if that means describing an uncle who used to steal from his customers as "a man who always looked for the best in others—and when he found it, he took it."

SURVIVAL POINTS

1. When sharing a story about a deceased loved one, remember that what you say reflects on you just as much as it does on her. Therefore, don't hesitate to refer to your abusive Aunt Kate as a "great, great man."

2. If you screw up and accidentally tell a story about how you and the deceased used to spend all day bird watching, only to learn that she was blind, another great way to cover your ass is by saying something like, "I guess you didn't know Aunt Magoo the way I did."

3. Every family has a relative who'll be *very* tough to describe in a positive light. If you're ever struggling to find a nice way to remember someone, just refer to him or her as "passionate." This means that whatever he did in this world, at least he cared about it. Even a mass murderer who ate his victims can be described as a "passionate people person."

chapter 37

WHO DIED AND MADE YOU BOSS?
(THROWING A KICK-ASS FUNERAL)

Death ends a life, not a relationship.

· ROBERT BENCHLEY ·

. . . Tell that to Nicole Brown Simpson.

Poor Grandpa Shmeckle has finally succumbed to old age (and his wife's nagging. What Shmeckle could take such a beating)? He lived a full, long, and happy life. And he was one of the most liked members of the family. It's time to remember him properly. It's time to have a funeral for Grandpa Shmeckle.

But say it was you who'd just kicked the bucket. How would you want your family to observe your passing? Do you want people to be relaxed and have fun, or do you want them to worry about whether or not they've gotten the right flowers, called or visited appropriately, made the proper condolences, and so on? To truly survive a funeral, we must consider changing the way in which a few things are done:

Hearing the Bad News

Old etiquette: You get the call relaying the sad news. At this moment, there are several opportunities when you can potentially screw the pooch (not literally—unless that's how you grieve). Should you call the bereaved? Should you visit the house and bring food? If you think that you're a "just call" relative, not showing up in person could create a rift in the family that may last until the next funeral (provided you aren't starring in it). No one wants to hear bad news, *and* play a "how close am I to the bereaved" guessing game.

New etiquette: The bereaved should just throw a killer party. He or she doesn't have to wait until the wake or reception to have a shindig. This way, there'll be plenty of company and food. Everyone will know to come over, and no one will fear having to be the sole comforter. There's no better way to announce someone's passing than telling the family, "We're sorry to announce that Grandpa died. Please come over for a preburial, backyard-bonfire party."

Attire

Old etiquette: Isn't wearing black clothes a little depressing? What's so respectful about plain, boring dark suits and dresses? This doesn't mean you should wear fru-fru clothes like a Care Bear T-shirt (even if the deceased's last moments were spent running from a grizzly, it may seem appropriate, but it's not). But there's got to be a better way to dress.

New etiquette: There's no celebration of life quite like a rave. Oversized pants, glow-sticks, baby pacifiers, and beads—that's what a real mourner wears to pay his respects. Wearing black says, "A part of me has also died." Would you want a part of *your* loved one to die? Absolutely not! Dressing like a college student with the ability to dance and a weekend drug habit says, "Thinking of you makes me want to groove until someone of the opposite sex is so overcome with exhaustion that she finds me attractive."

Flowers, Gifts, and Charitable Contributions

Old etiquette: Should you send flowers to the house or the funeral parlor? Should you buy a gift or make a charitable donation? Although the bereaved typically clarify what they'd like done, who wants to spend time picking out flowers or chipping in with siblings to buy the widow a bereavement cruise (conveniently ignoring the fact that her husband died in a freak shuffleboard accident)? Or what if Grandpa Shmeckle's favorite charity was Bullets for Boys, a program to teach inner-city youths that instead of shooting each other in gang fights, they should shoot deer and elk? Despite his wishes that a donation be made, you just can't see the wisdom in providing at-risk youths with artillery.

New etiquette: The way to avoid all this nonsense is to just have a PayPal account whereby people can go online and deposit money. It can then be used to buy flowers or gifts, or even funneled to a Basque separatists' group; whatever helps the healing.

Funeral Service/Graveside Service

Old etiquette: Unfortunately, this is a wonderful time to accidentally piss people off. Some relatives will be angry that the ceremony is at the funeral home instead of the church. Others are irate that the funeral wasn't held at the Golden Skate, the roller-skating rink where Grandpa Shmeckle first "shot the duck," and met Grandma Shmeckle. And religion rarely plays a bigger part in most families' lives than during funerals. Alas, it's an ideal opportunity to accidentally offend by not knowing the customs of *that* side of the family, or allowing a service to be performed that, were the deceased aware of it, would make him roll over in his grave.

New etiquette: The service should be a direct reflection of the deceased's personality and values. Was he a religious man? Then have a religious ceremony. But *announce* what the rules are. Technically, a Jew can think of himself as a very, very, very lapsed Catholic—and should do so to honor Cousin Mickey O'Shenanagen's memory. And tell non-Jews at a Jewish ceremony that no matter how sincere their intentions, saying "He's with Jesus now" isn't cool. And if Grandpa Shmeckle wasn't religious but loved to eat, why not afford him the honor of a hot dog–inspired funeral? All you need is a beige mattress folded around the casket to transform it into a hot dog. Nothing's more beautiful than hearing whoever's presiding over the ceremony say, "Here rests Grandpa Shmeckle, in the way he wanted to be remembered—as a giant, all-beef wiener."

The After Party (Wake/Reception)

Old etiquette: This part actually isn't so bad. Most folks have some kind of party to refresh themselves and remember the deceased. It's basically like a family reunion, except that it's been organized by a blocked artery, not Aunt Betty.

New etiquette: Again, there really isn't too much wrong with this part of the funeral experience. However, it would be a lot more fun if there were some games that helped everyone remember the deceased, like What Were Grandpa's Favorite Curse Words? Young kids especially love this game.

Many people naturally want to discuss their fondest memories of the deceased. Why not also play a fun guessing game? Have everyone write each of his or her fondest moments with Grandpa Shmeckle on a piece of paper, and put it in a hat. Mix them up, then read one while everyone tries to guess whose moment it is. Just be careful. If the memory is "The first time I made love to Shmeckle," and both his widow and her sister raise their hands, you might watch his widow suddenly break into her own game of Favorite Curse Words. In fact, that might inspire Grandma Shmeckle to plan another funeral.

WE'RE DYING TO HAVE A GOOD TIME

To properly honor the deceased, put on your flip-flops, play some Grateful Dead, and relax. And the next time *you* die, remember that being the guy who made your relatives get their suits dry-cleaned won't exactly get fresh flowers delivered to your gravesite.

SURVIVAL TIPS

1. It's always a good idea to bring food—unless the deceased died of obesity. That's like bringing a shotgun to Kurt Cobain's funeral.

2. Bereave it or not: In Asian religions, such as Buddhism and Hinduism, they believe in reincarnation. Therefore, when comforting the bereaved at one of these ceremonies, it's okay to say, "Don't worry. I'm sure Uncle Chan will be back shortly, in the form of an orangutan or your sister's love child."

3. If you're a traditionalist and can't see the wisdom of dressing in rave pajamas, you can still wear black—but mix up the kinds of clothes. Wear black jeans and a black jean jacket with black leather chaps, or even an all-black NASCAR racing unitard. Or if you really want to get into the festivities, you can even wear a black hood and carry a scythe!

PART

×III

OH NO YOU DI-IN'T!
(SURVIVING FEUDS, FIGHTS, AND REALLY CRAZY SHIT)

chapter 38

WHEN TO TALK ABOUT ABORTION
(AND OTHER TECHNIQUES FOR BRINGING ABOUT CIVIL DISCOURSE)

The inappropriate cannot be beautiful.

· FRANK LLOYD WRIGHT ·

. . . But it can be a lot of fun.

.

We all have family members who will try to bring up inappropriate topics during a meal, or at any time during a family visit when they think they can get away with it. Some uncle will drink just enough to try talking about blow jobs during Christmas dinner. Then he'll slur out some defense like, "What? The kids are eleven and twelve; they'll know what blow jobs are soon enough."

When a relative blurts out something that's so rude, wrong, raunchy, or racist that he even sets *your* family on edge, we have two main defenses: sarcasm and segues.

No, I'm Not being Sarcastic at All

Imagine the scenario: You and your family are gathered around the table, comparing the ages at which each of you lost your virginity (you know—normal family discourse). The conversation is pleasant, happy, and comfortable. Then out of nowhere, some relative asks your personal opinion on sodomy. Bang! Just like that, a conversation-destroying dirty bomb was lobbed onto the dinner table. Your family's sitting in stunned silence. Even your sister has stopped talking (which is almost as shocking as the comment itself). The topic may be suitable for the champagne room at Déjà Vu, but has no place when eating on fine china.

So what can you do to carefully cut the red and blue wires in that relative's comment? Simply stand up and say, "I want to talk about abortion! Screw sodomy. I want to argue that even though Uncle Bill has yet to 'get a life,' it nonetheless still begins at conception!" This over-the-top sarcastic response mocks the sodomy-inquiring relative. You've one-upped him. Now the family can laugh off the uncomfortable situation and move on to a normal topic, like how to jam police radar by putting tinfoil balls in the hubcaps of your car. (If, however, someone does try to bring up abortion, you must then substitute child slavery, female circumcision, or any other appropriately offensive subject.)

Speaking of Motor Oil, who wants Coffee?

We can also employ a less aggressive approach to moving mealtime away from taboo subjects. You may have a born-again aunt who cringes even when NASA mentions they're aborting a space flight. If absurdly over-the-top comments may potentially cause more harm than good, then let's use a handful of fun, conversation-changing segues.

For example, if dear, ninety-year-old Grandma Clovis has found her way back to the speakeasy, and has begun calling her late husband a "homo" between hiccups, just stand and interrupt with, "Who wants seconds?" or "Who wants dessert?"

The key to using a segue is that it must not appear to have any connection to the taboo subject being broached. If your mother-in-law decides it's time to tell the story of how she found out about the slut her ex-husband was having an affair with, don't say, "It's time for dessert. Who wants a tart?" Hearing her entire family answer, "Yes, I'd love a tart!" might be too much for her to handle.

Also, choose a segue that you think will provoke a response from more than one relative. If your brother doesn't know better than to tell the entire extended family that he got busted during his senior year in high school for selling acid, don't cut him off with, "Has anyone been to the movies lately?" If no one's recently been, your question may just hang there. Even worse, that brother might say, "I just saw the *Lion King* in 3-D. It was a trip." You're better off asking, "Who here has thumbs?" Even though it's nonsense, your entire family (except poor, thumbless Suzie, who recently sold her meat slicer on eBay) should say, "I do! I do!"

I MISSED WHAT YOU SAID—SOMEONE ELSE WAS TALKING

Not every family visit will be brought to a screeching halt by an inappropriate comment. But in those instances when your dad asks your sister's new boyfriend if it's still acceptable to refer to him as a mulatto, you'll be thankful that you've got an outrageous, sarcastic comeback to shock the conversation back into bounds. And when out of nowhere, your uncle asks your niece if she's gay, just remember not to ask, "Would anyone like dessert? I've got ladyfingers."

SURVIVAL TIPS

1. Don't dread having a relative present who's known to make off-color remarks. These people are no different than those with hereditary genes for obesity or early hair loss: every family's got them, and science is doing all it can to find a cure.

2. Alcohol consumption usually precedes an inappropriate statement— someone who's slurring is about to make a slur.

3. The only time you *wouldn't* want to shock the conversation out of the danger zone is when the person who's being offended has it coming. Your sister-in-law just threatened to slit your tires if you bought a Hummer. If your uncle follows by asking her, "What have you got against *Hummers*? Don't you ever want to get married?" it will definitely be inappropriate. But it's also karma.

chapter 39

WHAT TO DO WHEN YOUR MOM GETS DRUNK AND CALLS YOUR WIFE A WHORE

(AND OTHER TECHNIQUES FOR HANDLING REALLY CRAZY SHIT)

Truly great madness cannot be achieved
without significant intelligence.

· HENRIK TIKKANEN ·

. . . Well, in that case, bipolar Aunt Betty
must be smart as hell.

No family visit is complete unless someone's been brought to tears. It's practically tradition. In fact, many of our fondest family memories are times when there's been yelling matches, fistfights, and meltdowns. No one cares about family visits that are smooth, uneventful, and joyous. But when your Aunt Petunia, still traumatized from all the times her older sister would "forget" to set her a place at the table, soils herself in protest to having to sit on a metal folding chair during dinner, you've got a story that can be passed down for generations.

But some of us may not know what to do when our family visit is blessed with a crying fit, thrown dish, name-calling, or brawl. No matter how dysfunctional we think our family is, something can always happen that even goes beyond the usual level of expected behavior.

The question is, how do we respond when something happens at the family visit that's one video camera away from being an episode of *Cops?*

THE ATTITUDE OF GRATITUDE

First of all, be thankful. Major fights and meltdowns are opportunities for the family to grow. For example, let's say your mom finally summons the courage to call your wife a whore. It's something she's wanted to say since your wedding. Through the magic of the holidays, she finally feels close enough to her to explain how she feels. Don't get angry at your mom's verbal assault! Just look on the bright side: they're finally talking. That's an improvement right there. Now that there's a dialogue, you can defend your wife in a way that brings the two women closer together. Calling your mom a psycho or a drunk will just hurt her feelings. But saying something like, "Well, I married her because she reminds me of you" will help the two ladies see what they've got in common.

MELTDOWNS

When a relative "loses her shit," it's also an opportunity for the family to learn a little more about themselves. If a cousin, brother, or aunt implodes for no apparent reason, it's as though they've bravely chosen to embody all the various mental illnesses of your gene pool at once.

But one must be careful when a family member decides to go Chernobyl. If bipolar Aunt Betty starts to cry and smash dishes because her nine-year-old nephew doesn't like the Ann Coulter book she's gotten him for Christmas, you'd better find shelter from her emotional tornado. One must survive an event to grow from it. Should you mistakenly ask, "What made you think a nine-year-old would want a book about politics?" there isn't a basement in Kansas that would keep you safe from all the teacups about to be hurled at your head.

Once the meltdown has ended and Aunt Betty is either sleeping off her insanity or manically asking the kids if they'd like to go out for ice cream, it's safe to emerge from your shelter. You and your family can then discuss her antics. Most of you will walk away with a lesson about what happens when you don't get your omega-3s, order too many lattes, or otherwise let your body chemistry come within an adrenal gland of turning you into the Hulk.

A relative who has a meltdown is like a family science project. We get to stand back and watch what happens when too much dry ice is added to the volcano.

FISTFIGHTS

Fistfights are like ballet—a physical expression of emotions (although a performance of *The Nutcracker* may mean a trip to the hospital, not to mention getting on the waiting list at an adoption agency). Brawls are poetry in motion, and when they occur among relatives, it's another opportunity for the family to explore the conflicts that make them who they are. And just like a gang initiation requires a "beat down," the two relatives who come to blows will have a special connection that will last as long as they're willing to talk to each other. Let's look at how to appreciate a family fistfight:

1. When it erupts, the first thing you should do is open the front door and yell, "You'd better stop. I've called the cops!" That way, if a neighbor hears the ruckus, he won't call the cops, believing that you already have. You don't want outsiders ruining this special family moment.

2. Then, the entire family should form a circle around the warring parties and take sides. Even if it's a wrestling match between two kids who both want to play with the same Tonka truck, come together and form a ring. This will make the fight easier to watch, and keep the tots from grabbing beer bottles to break over each other's heads.

3. Next, encourage the fighters. Yelling things like, "Kick his ass, Uncle Al!" or "Rip that bitch's hair out, Jennifer!" will let a family member know that you've got his or her back. Whoever you're pulling for needs your support. Remember, self-esteem starts in the home.

4. Finishing what one starts is an important family virtue. Therefore, if it appears that both of the combatants want to call a truce, be sure to yell, "Don't stop! Finish him, Jimmy! You can stop fighting when it's time for dessert, and not a second earlier."

5. Once the fight's over, be sure to comfort the loser by saying, "Don't worry about it, Michelle. You'll kick her ass next Christmas."

I DEMAND A REMATCH

Crazy stuff will happen at family visits. Rather than letting these events scar us for life, fistfights, meltdowns, and verbal attacks should be appreciated as opportunities to learn about ourselves and bring folks together.

If next year, your dad accuses your uncle of having had an affair with your mom, don't get nervous—get excited that you've finally got an answer as to why you have your uncle's eyes.

SURVIVAL TIPS

1. Don't worry if young kids get into fistfights. Brawling burns a lot of calories and is a good prevention against childhood obesity.

2. Witnessing a relative's meltdown is also great preventative medicine. Nothing will encourage you to keep attending yoga classes like seeing a grown man cry because the Christmas tree's crooked.

3. While all fights are special, try to encourage fisticuffs over important issues. Sometimes, beating the shit out of each other is the only way in which two female relatives can deal with the fact that they've both worn the same dress.

PART

xIV

CONCLUSION

chapter 40

Only You Can Prevent Forest Fires

Once upon a time, in a magical forest by the sea ever lathering, it was again time for a family gathering.

All the uncle bears were telling each other about boring stuff from bear work, and cousin squirrels were running around the forest house, going quite berserk.

Mama Mongoose was drinking malt liquor as she fought with her husband the Ferret. And he had had about enough of her crap, and was making eyes at a distant-cousin parrot.

Soon they all sat down for dinner, and one of the step-bear dads said, "I want you all to know well enough, that for ten years I've come to this boring family gathering and eaten the exact same stuff.

"Is it just me who thinks the food is all rather plain? I'd rather eat honey off the end of a hunter's shotgun than eat this crap again."

At this, the hostess, Mrs. Hedgehog, became thoroughly pissed. She stood on her chair and shook her little hedgehog fist.

"Apologize right now, you son-of-a-bear bitch! Or I'll tell the family what you don't want them to know—that you lost your job three weeks ago!

"You still leave the house every day, but all you do is hang out at the bear arcade."

At this news, all his wolf brothers began to howl and bark. Then Hedgehog cleared her voice and asked, "Who wants turkey? I've got white meat and dark."

"Eat whatever you like," Step-Dad Bear began to spout. "Her food's so bad that even Bulimic Beaver won't need her finger to barf it back out."

And at that, the magical forest went silent.

Mama Mongoose looked very angry and surprised, and shot unemployed Step-Bear a stare with her mongoose-bitch eyes.

She'd had it up to her whiskers with the way her family acted. It was just about time that someone reacted.

The mongoose ran about the forest floor collecting lots of twigs, and set them about her family, while taking malt-liquor swigs.

Then to a nearby car she ran really fast, shimmied up the rear fender and siphoned out some gas.

And just as she was about to strike the match and end this awful stewing, a young squirrel cousin saw her and asked, "Mama Mongoose, what the hell are you doing?"

"I can't take it any more!" Mama Mongoose squealed. "I can't remember the last time we had a nice family meal!

"And now with one match, all of your asses can go have your family gathering with the greenhouse gases!"

The young squirrel listened to Mongoose's plight. And then he said, "Please wait a moment. I may have a better idea instead."

The squirrel considered the problem his family had: seeing each other drove them extremely mad.

Then by the light of the moon in which to confide, he created for them *Relative Discomfort: The Family Survival Guide.*

He returned to the gathering with not a second to spare, and said to them all, even fighting Mama's stare:

"Hey, family! Quit being lame. Read this book; during family visits, it'll help keep you sane."

And so his family read the book. And Step-Bear apologized to Hedgehog the cook.

Ferret and Mongoose made their amends, and Ferret promised that he and the parrot were just friends.

Everyone smiled and laughed, and enjoyed the dinner—even if it tasted worse than paint thinner.

And the forest was once again peaceful, and happiness could now abound (until about a month later, when an arsonist burned the forest to the ground).

And it is with this joyous tale that our little journey ends. Please be good to your family, and treat them as though they were your friends.

Please give your mom the benefit of the doubt when, for no reason, she starts to shout.

Please take it easy if your daughter should marry into a family, that's kinda sleazy and scary.

Please laugh, no matter what your relatives do. Hopefully, they'll do the same when you annoy them, too.

The End.

Acknowledgments

First and foremost, I would like to thank my wonderful agent, Elise Proulx—for everything; with an incredible debt of thanks to Lane Butler, for loving the book and providing her wonderful spirit, guidance, and editing talents; let me also thank all the other great people at Andrews McMeel who helped put this bad boy together and who dig the same stuff I do; and very special thanks for the blessed friendship of Chris Federico—who taught me how to spell my name. Without him, there'd be no me.

I also want to give infinite thanks Andrew Norelli, for his brotherhood and friendship since back in the old country; to Tommy Savitt, for personifying chutzpah; to Steve Cvengros, Cassandra Douglas, and Craig Playstead, for letting me through; to Chris "Sandy" Sanders, for making Chicago feel like home; to Hilary Sares, for talking to me— your black eye was one of the best things to happen in my life; to Clint Berquist, for having kick-ass equipment and the talent to use it; to Melik, for tricking me into buying his girlfriend dinner; to Steve "the Ointment" Tatham, for having a great show; to Jordan Lindstrom, for living where I do; and to Larry Getlen, for actually reading it.

And for the love and support of my family: Mom, Dad, Jon, with extra props to Lauren (what's an NYU English degree have that I don't?); to Arlene and all her offspring; to Ryann and Ethan; and to Dagny, my dog, and what's left of my dear old cat, Meow-Meow.

Let me as well thank all the great bookers, club owners, agencies, and friends who first gave my stand-up a place to stand. It's impossible to name you all, but extra special thanks must be given to Bert Haas, John Yoder, Mark Kolo, Chuck Wozlick, Pamela Whitehead, Julie Mains, Jeff Johnson, and Jon Fox.

And finally, let me give great thanks to you: the reader! I've got to go, but let me give you a call later.

Jeremy Greenberg is a writer and comic born in New York, raised in the Bay Area, and currently making his home in Seattle. He has been a contributor to *The Complete Idiot's Guide to Jokes* (Alpha/Penguin) and a contributing joke writer for *Comics Unleashed with Byron Allen.* This is his first book.

When Jeremy isn't writing or traveling the globe performing stand-up, he is at home with his wife. Learn more at www.jeremygreenberg.com.